Data Analysis with Stata

Explore the big data field and learn how to perform data analytics and predictive modeling in Stata

Prasad Kothari

 enterprise

professional expertise distilled

PUBLISHING

BIRMINGHAM - MUMBAI

Data Analysis with Stata

First published: October 2015

Production reference: 1231015

Published by Packt Publishing Ltd.
Livery Place
35 Livery Street
Birmingham B3 2PB, UK.

ISBN 978-1-78217-317-5

www.packtpub.com

Credits

Author
Prasad Kothari

Reviewers
Aspen Chen
Roberto Ferrer
Levicatus Mugenyi

Commissioning Editor
Taron Pereira

Acquisition Editor
Meeta Rajani

Content Development Editor
Priyanka Mehta

Technical Editor
Tejaswita Karvir

Copy Editor
Stuti Srivastava

Project Coordinator
Mary Alex

Proofreader
Safis Editing

Indexer
Priya Sane

Graphics
Abhinash Sahu

Production Coordinator
Shantanu N. Zagade

Cover Work
Shantanu N. Zagade

About the Author

Prasad Kothari is an analytics thought leader. He has worked extensively with organizations such as Merck, Sanofi Aventis, Freddie Mac, Fractal Analytics, and the National Institute of Health on various analytics and big data projects. He has published various research papers in the American Journal of Drug and Alcohol Abuse and American Public Health Association.

Prasad is an industrial engineer from V.J.T.I. and has done his MS in management information systems from the University of Arizona. He works closely with different labs at MIT on digital analytics projects and research.

He has worked extensively on many statistical tools, such as R, Stata, SAS, SPSS, and Python. His leadership and analytics skills have been pivotal in setting up analytics practices for various organizations and helping them in growing across the globe.

Prasad set up a fraud investigation team at Freddie Mac, which is a world-renowned team, and has been known in the fraud-detection industry as a pioneer in cutting-edge analytical techniques. He also set up a sales forecasting team at Merck and Sanofi Aventis and helped these pharmaceutical companies discover new groundbreaking analytical techniques for drug discovery and clinical trials. Prasad also worked with the US government (the healthcare department at NIH) and consulted them on various healthcare analytics projects. He played pivotal role in ObamaCare.

You can find out about healthcare social media management and analytics at http://www.amazon.in/Healthcare-Social-Media-Management-Analytics-ebook/dp/B00VPZFOGE/ref=sr_1_1?s=digital-text&ie=UTF8&qid=1439376295&sr=1-1.

About the Reviewers

Aspen Chen is a doctoral candidate in sociology at the University of Connecticut. His primary research areas are education, immigration, and social stratification. He is currently completing his dissertation on early educational trajectories of U.S. immigrant children. The statistical programs that Aspen uses include Stata, R, SPSS, SAS, and M-Plus. His Stata routine, available at the Statistical Software Components (SSC) repertoire, calculates quasi-variances.

Roberto Ferrer is an economist with a general interest in computer programming and a particular interest in statistical programming. He has developed his professional career in central banking, contributing with his research in the Bureau of Economic Research at Venezuela's Central Bank. He uses Stata on a daily basis and contributes regularly to Statalist, a forum moderated by Stata users and maintained by StataCorp. He is also a regular at Stack Overflow, where he answers questions under the `Stata` tag.

Levicatus Mugenyi is a Ugandan, who was born in the Rakai district. He has 9 years of experience in handling health research data. He started his professional career as a data manager in 2005 after successfully completing his bachelor's degree in statistics from Makerere University Kampala, Uganda. In 2008, he was awarded a scholarship by the Flemish government to undertake a master's degree in biostatistics from Hasselt University, Belgium. After successfully completing the master's program with a distinction, he rejoined Infectious Diseases Research Collaboration (IDRC) and Uganda Malaria Surveillance Project (UMSP) as a statistician in 2010. In 2013, he was awarded an ICP PhD sandwich scholarship on a research project titled *Estimation of infectious disease parameters for transmission of malaria in Ugandan children*. His research interests include stochastic and deterministic modeling of infectious diseases, survival data analysis, and longitudinal/clustered data analysis. In addition, he enjoys teaching statistical methods. He is also a director and a senior consultant at the Levistat statistical consultancy based in Uganda. His long-term goal is to provide evidence-based information to improve the management of infectious diseases, including malaria, HIV/AIDS, and tuberculosis, in Uganda as well as Africa.

He is currently employed at Hasselt University, Belgium. He was formerly employed (part time) at Infectious Diseases Research Collaboration (IDRC), Kampala, Uganda. He owns a company called Levistat Statistical Consultancy, Uganda.

www.PacktPub.com

Support files, eBooks, discount offers, and more

For support files and downloads related to your book, please visit www.PacktPub.com.

Did you know that Packt offers eBook versions of every book published, with PDF and ePub files available? You can upgrade to the eBook version at www.PacktPub.com and as a print book customer, you are entitled to a discount on the eBook copy. Get in touch with us at service@packtpub.com for more details.

At www.PacktPub.com, you can also read a collection of free technical articles, sign up for a range of free newsletters and receive exclusive discounts and offers on Packt books and eBooks.

https://www2.packtpub.com/books/subscription/packtlib

Do you need instant solutions to your IT questions? PacktLib is Packt's online digital book library. Here, you can search, access, and read Packt's entire library of books.

Why subscribe?

- Fully searchable across every book published by Packt
- Copy and paste, print, and bookmark content
- On demand and accessible via a web browser

Free access for Packt account holders

If you have an account with Packt at www.PacktPub.com, you can use this to access PacktLib today and view 9 entirely free books. Simply use your login credentials for immediate access.

Instant updates on new Packt books

Get notified! Find out when new books are published by following @PacktEnterprise on Twitter or the *Packt Enterprise* Facebook page.

Table of Contents

Preface

This book covers data management, visualization of graphs, and programming in Stata. Starting with an introduction to Stata and data analytics, you'll move on to Stata programming and data management. The book also takes you through data visualization and all the important statistical tests in Stata. Linear and logistic regression in Stata is covered as well. As you progress, you will explore a few analyses, including survey analysis, time series analysis, and survival analysis in Stata. You'll also discover different types of statistical modeling techniques and learn how to implement these techniques in Stata. This book will be provided with a code bundle, but the readers would have to build their own datasets as they proceed with the chapters.

What this book covers

Chapter 1, *An Introduction to Stata and Data Analytics*, gives an overview of Stata programming and the various statistical models that can be built in Stata.

Chapter 2, *Stata Programming and Data Management*, teaches you how to manage data by changing labels, how to create new variables, and how to replace existing variables and make them better from the modeling perspective. It also discusses how to drop and keep important variables for the analysis, how to summarize the data tables into report formats, and how to append or merge different data files. Finally, it teaches you how to prepare reports and prepare the data for further graphs and modeling assignments.

Chapter 3, *Data Visualization*, discusses scatter plots, histograms, and various graphing techniques, and the nitty-gritty involved in the visualization of data in Stata. It showcases how to perform visualization in Stata through code and graphical interfaces. Both are equally effective ways to create graphs and visualizations.

Chapter 4, *Important Statistical Tests in Stata*, discusses how statistical tests, such as t-tests, chi square tests, ANOVA, MANOVA, and Fisher's test, are significant in terms of the model-building exercise. The more tests you conduct on the given data, the better an understanding you will have of the data, and you can check how different variables interact with each other in the data.

Chapter 5, *Linear Regression in Stata*, teaches you linear regression methods and their assumptions. You also get a review of all the nitty-gritty, such as multicollinearity, homoscedasticity, and so on.

Chapter 6, *Logistic Regression in Stata*, covers how to build a logistic regression model and what the best business situations in which such a model can be applied are. It also teaches you the theory and application aspects of logistic regression.

Chapter 7, *Survey Analysis in Stata*, teaches you different sampling concepts and methods. You also learn how to implement these methods in Stata and how to apply statistical modeling concepts, such as regression to the survey data.

Chapter 8, *Time Series Analysis in Stata*, covers time series concepts, such as seasonality, cyclic behavior of the data, and autoregression and moving averages methods. You also learn how to apply these concepts in Stata and how to conduct various statistical tests to make sure that the time series analysis that you performed is correct.

Chapter 9, *Survival Analysis in Stata*, teaches survival analysis and different statistical concepts associated with it in detail.

What you need for this book

For this book, you need any version of the Stata software.

Who this book is for

This book is for all professionals and students who want to learn Stata programming and apply predictive modeling concepts. It is also very helpful for experienced Stata programmers, as it provides information about advanced statistical modeling concepts and their application.

Conventions

In this book, you will find a number of text styles that distinguish between different kinds of information. Here are some examples of these styles and an explanation of their meaning.

Code words in text, database table names, folder names, filenames, file extensions, pathnames, dummy URLs, user input, and Twitter handles are shown as follows: "We can include other contexts through the use of the `include` directive."

A block of code is set as follows:

```
infix dictionary using Survey2010.dat
{
  dta
  rowtype  1-2
  yr  3-4 quart5 [...]
}
```

Any command-line input or output is written as follows:

```
assert popscon>0,

assert popscon<0
```

New terms and **important words** are shown in bold. Words that you see on the screen, for example, in menus or dialog boxes, appear in the text like this: " You can also select the **Reporting** tab and select the **Report estimated coefficients** option."

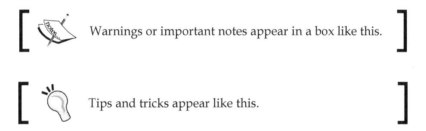

Warnings or important notes appear in a box like this.

Tips and tricks appear like this.

Reader feedback

Feedback from our readers is always welcome. Let us know what you think about this book—what you liked or disliked. Reader feedback is important for us as it helps us develop titles that you will really get the most out of.

To send us general feedback, simply e-mail feedback@packtpub.com, and mention the book's title in the subject of your message.

If there is a topic that you have expertise in and you are interested in either writing or contributing to a book, see our author guide at www.packtpub.com/authors.

Customer support

Now that you are the proud owner of a Packt book, we have a number of things to help you to get the most from your purchase.

Downloading the example code

You can download the example code files from your account at `http://www.packtpub.com` for all the Packt Publishing books you have purchased. If you purchased this book elsewhere, you can visit `http://www.packtpub.com/support` and register to have the files e-mailed directly to you.

Downloading the color images of this book

We also provide you with a PDF file that has color images of the screenshots/ diagrams used in this book. The color images will help you better understand the changes in the output. You can download this file from `http://www.packtpub.com/sites/default/files/downloads/1234OT_ColorImages.pdf`.

Errata

Although we have taken every care to ensure the accuracy of our content, mistakes do happen. If you find a mistake in one of our books — maybe a mistake in the text or the code — we would be grateful if you could report this to us. By doing so, you can save other readers from frustration and help us improve subsequent versions of this book. If you find any errata, please report them by visiting `http://www.packtpub.com/submit-errata`, selecting your book, clicking on the **Errata Submission Form** link, and entering the details of your errata. Once your errata are verified, your submission will be accepted and the errata will be uploaded to our website or added to any list of existing errata under the Errata section of that title.

To view the previously submitted errata, go to `https://www.packtpub.com/books/content/support` and enter the name of the book in the search field. The required information will appear under the **Errata** section.

Piracy

Piracy of copyrighted material on the Internet is an ongoing problem across all media. At Packt, we take the protection of our copyright and licenses very seriously. If you come across any illegal copies of our works in any form on the Internet, please provide us with the location address or website name immediately so that we can pursue a remedy.

Please contact us at `copyright@packtpub.com` with a link to the suspected pirated material.

We appreciate your help in protecting our authors and our ability to bring you valuable content.

Questions

If you have a problem with any aspect of this book, you can contact us at `questions@packtpub.com`, and we will do our best to address the problem.

1
Introduction to Stata and Data Analytics

These days, many people use Stata for econometric and medical research purposes, among other things. There are many people who use different packages, such as **Statistical Package for the Social Sciences (SPSS)** and EViews, Micro, RATS/CATS (used by time series experts), and R for Matlab/Guass/Fortan (used for hardcore analysis). One should know the usage of Stata and then apply it in one's relative fields. Stata is a command-driven language; there are over 500 different commands and menu options, and each has a particular syntax required to invoke any of the various options. Learning these commands is a time-consuming process, but it is not hard. At the end of each class, your do-file will contain all the commands that we have covered, but there is no way we will cover all of these commands in this short introductory course.

Stata is a combined statistical analytical tool that is intended for use by research scholars and analytics practitioners. Stata has many strengths, but we are going to talk about the most important one: managing, adjusting, and arranging large sets of data. Stata has many versions, and with every version, it keeps on improving; for example, in Stata versions 11 to 14, there are changes and progress in the computing speed, capabilities and functionalities, as well as flexible graphic capabilities. Over a period of time, Stata keeps on changing and updating the model as per users' suggestions. In short, the regression method is based on a nonstandard feature, which means that you can easily get help from the Web if another person has written a program that can be integrated with their software for the purpose of analysis. The following topics will be covered in this chapter:

- Introducing Data analytics
- Introducing the Stata interface and basic techniques

Introducing data analytics

We analyze data everyday for various reasons. To predict an event or forecast the key indicators, such as the revenue for a given organization, is fast becoming a major requirement in the industry. There are various types of techniques and tools that can be leveraged to analyze the data. Here are the techniques that will be covered in this book using Stata as a tool:

- **Stata programming and data management**: Before predicting anything, we need to manage and massage the data in order to make it good enough to be something through which insights can be derived. The programming aspect helps in creating new variables to treat data in such a way that finding patterns in historical data or predicting the outcome of given event becomes much easier.

- **Data visualization**: After the data preparation, we need to visualize the data for the the following:
  - To view what patterns in the data look like
  - To check whether there are any outliers in the data
  - To understand the data better
  - To draw preliminary insights from the data

- **Important statistical tests in Stata**: After data visualization, based on observations, you can try to come up with various hypotheses about the data. We need to test these hypotheses on the datasets to check whether they are statistically significant and whether we can depend on and apply these hypotheses in future situations as well.

- **Linear regression in Stata**: Once done with the hypothesis testing, there is always a business need to predict one of the variables, such as what the revenue of the financial organization will be in specific conditions, and so on. These predictions about continuous variables, such as revenue, the default amount on a credit card, and the number of items sold in a given store, come through linear regression. Linear regression is the most basic and widely used prediction methodology. We will go into details of linear regression in a later chapter.

- **Logistic regression in Stata**: When you need to predict the outcome of a particular event along with the probability, logistic regression is the best and most acknowledged method by far. Predicting which team will win the match in football or cricket or predicting whether a customer will default on a loan payment can be decided through the probabilities given by logistic regression.

- **Survey analysis in Stata**: Understanding the customer sentiment and consumer experience is one of the biggest requirements of the retail industry. The research industry also needs data about people's opinions in order to derive the effect of a certain event or the sentiments of the affected people. All of these can be achieved by conducting and analyzing survey datasets. Survey analysis can have various subtechniques, such as factor analysis, principle component analysis, panel data analysis, and so on.

- **Time series analysis in Stata**: When you try to forecast a time-dependent variable with reasonable cyclic behavior of seasonality, time series analysis comes handy. There are many techniques of time series analysis, but we will talk about a couple of them: **Autoregressive Integrated Moving Average (ARIMA)** and Box Jenkins. Forecasting the amount of rainfall depending on the amount of rainfall in the past 5 years is a classic time series analysis problem.

- **Survival analysis in Stata**: These days, lots of customers attrite from telecom plans, healthcare plans, and so on, and join the competitors. When you need to develop a churn model or attrition model to check who will attrite, survival analysis is the best model.

The Stata interface

Let's discuss the location and layout of Stata. It is very easy to locate Stata on a computer or laptop: after installing the software, go to the start menu, go to the search menu, and type Stata. You can find the path where the file is saved. This depends on which version has been installed. Another way to find Stata on the computer is through the quick launch button as well as through **Start** programs.

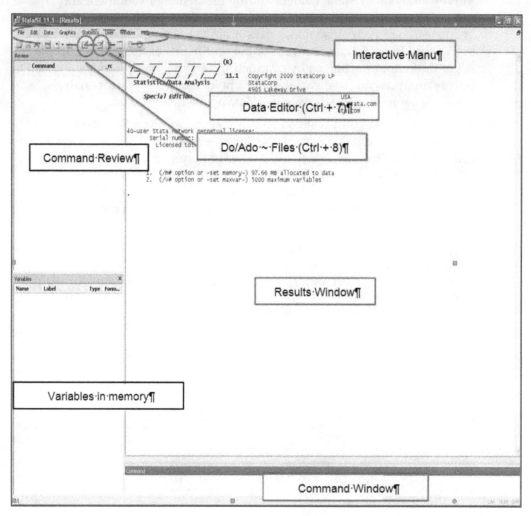

The preceding diagram represents the Stata layout. The four types of processors in Stata are multiprocessor (two or four), special edition processor (flavors), intercooled, and small processor. The multiprocessor is one of the most efficient processors. Though all processor versions function in a similar fashion, only the variables' repressors frequency increases with each new version. At present, Stata version 11 is in demand and is being used on various computers. It is a type of software that runs on commands. In the new versions of Stata, new ways, such as menus that can search Stata, have come in the market; however, typing a command is the simplest and quickest way to learn Stata. The more you use the functionality of typing the command, the better your understanding becomes. Through the typing technique, programming becomes easy and simple for analytics. Sometimes, it is difficult to find the exact syntax in commands; therefore, it is advisable that the menu command be used. Later on, you just copy the same command for further use. There are three ways to enter the commands, as follows:

- Use the do-file program. This is a type of program in which one has to inform the computer (through a command) that it needs to use the do-file type.
- Type the command manually.
- Enter the command interactively; just click on the menu screen.

Though all the three types discussed in the preceding bullets are used, the do-file type is the most frequently used one. The reason is that for a bigger file, it is faster as compared to manual typing. Secondly, it can store the data and keep it in the same format in which it was stored. Suppose you make a mistake and want to rectify it; what would you do? In this case, the do-file is useful; one can correct it and run the program again. Generally, an interactive command is used to find out the problem and later on, a do-file is used to solve it. The following is an example of an interactive command:

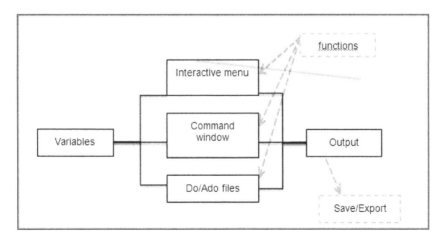

Data-storing techniques in Stata

Stata is a multipurpose program, which can serve not only its own data, but also other data in a simple format, for example, ASCII. Regardless of the data type format (Excel/statistical package), it gets automatically exported to the ASCII file. This means that all the data can now easily be imported to Stata.

The data entered in Stata is in different types of variables, such as vectors with individual observations in every row; it also holds strings and numeric strings. Every row has a detailed observation of the individual, country, firm, or whatever information is entered in Stata.

As the data is stored in variables, it makes Stata the most efficient way to store information. Sometimes, it is better to save the data in a different storage form, such as the following:

- Matrices
- Macros

Matrices should be used carefully as they consume more memory than variables, so there might be a possibility of low space memory before work is started.

Another form is **macros**; these are similar to variables in other programming languages and are named containers, which means they contain information of any type. There are two flavors of macros: local/temporary and global. **Global macros** are flexible and easy to manage; once they are defined in a computer or laptop, they can be easily opened through all commands. On the other hand, **local macros** are temporary objects that are formed for a particular environment and cannot be used in another area. For example, if you use a local macro for a do-file, that code will only exist in that particular environment.

Directories and folders in Stata

Stata has a tree-style structure to organize directories as well as folders similar to other operating systems, such as Windows, Linux, Unix, and Mac OS. This makes things easy and folders can be retrieved later on dates that are convenient. For example, the data folder is used to save entire datasets, subfolders for every single dataset, and so on. In Stata, the following commands can be leveraged:

- Dos
- Linux
- Unix

For example, if you need to change the directory, you can use the CD command, as follows:

```
CD C:\Stataforlder
```

You can also generate a new directory along with the current directory you have been using. For example:

```
mkdir "newstata".
```

You can leverage the dir command to get the details of the directory. If you need the current directory name along with the directory, you can utilize the pwd or CD command.

The use of paths in Stata depends on the type of data. Usually, there are two paths: absolute and relative. The absolute path contains the full address, denoting the folder. In the command you have seen in the earlier example, we leveraged the CD command using the path that is absolute. On the contrary, the relative path provides us with the location of the file. The following example of mkdir has used the relative path:

```
mkdir "E\Stata|Stata1"
```

The use of the relative path will be beneficial, especially when working on different devices, such as a PC at home or a library or server. To separate folders, Windows and Dos use a backslash (\), whereas Linux and Unix use a slash (/). Sometimes, these connotations might be troublesome when working on the server where Stata is installed. As a general rule, it is advisable that you use slashes in the relative path as Stata can easily understand a slash as a separator. The following is an example of this:

```
mkdir "/Stata1/Data" - this is how you create the new folder for your
STATA work.
```

Reading data in Stata

Whenever data is inserted in Stata, it's copied into the RAM memory of the computer. Generally, some of the changes are not on the permanent side and are not saved. So, these changes are lost when you reopen the Stata session. You can enter the data into Stata in various ways. One of the most effective way is as follows:

```
Use E:\Stata1\t1 less  India pwt  80-2010.dta,  clear
```

The option at the end of the code, clear, makes Stata read the dataset again before you open another data file.

Another option with limited variables in the dataset is as follows:

```
use  country  year  using  "t1  less India  pwt  80-2010 . dta" ,  clear
```

Insheet

In order to read data in Stata, it has to be converted into a format other than Excel. Also, save the data in one of the following formats:

- Excel
- **CSV (comma separated values)**
- Text (where the delimiter is a **tab** or **comma**)

You need to take into consideration certain rules and regulations while working on Stata:

- Suppose that the first row in the Excel file contains the name of the variables or headers, that is, the sheet contains variable names (series/code/names). Then, the second row must have data. The title of the first row must be removed before saving the file.

- In Stata, every single word is read; therefore, any additional lines below or to the right of the data, for example, footnotes or endnotes, should be deleted before saving it. If essential, delete the entire bottom row or the column on the right-hand side.

- You should not put numbers in the beginning of the variable name. In Stata, a problem might occur when the file is arranged with years (1980, 1985) in the top row. In such cases, placing an underscore before numbers will be helpful, and this can be done by selecting the row, using the spreadsheet package, and finding replace tools; for example, 1980 becomes `_1980`, and so on.

- The most important thing to note is the deletion of commas from the data because Stata won't be able to understand the starting point and finishing point of columns and rows. You can do this by leveraging the *first find then replace* option.

- Notations such as double dots (. .) or hyphens (-) might trouble Stata and will create confusion because Stata can read a single dot (.) as double dots or hyphens as text.

After saving the data in the CSV format, it can be read in Stata, as shown in the following code snippet:

```
insheet using "E:\Stata1|t1 less India pwt 80-2010. txt", clear
```

If any changes are made to the data by applying the CD command, then it can be read as follows:

```
insheet using "t1 less India pwt 80-2010. txt", clear
```

Many ways are available for the `insheet` command. Options are defined as additional qualities of standard commands, which are generally added once the command ends, should have commas in between, and so on. The following are some of the options used in Stata:

- **The `clear` option**: This can be used to insert a new file, `insheet`, regardless of the selected data: `insheet using "E:\ Stata1\t1 less India pwt 80-2010 . txt" , clear`

- **The option name**: This provides insights of data (usually from the first row), which helps Stata remember the file automatically. However, in certain cases, if this option does not work, then Stata uses variable names; an example is as follows:

  ```
  insheet using "E:\Stata1 classes\t1 less India pwt 80-2010 . txt" , names  clear
  ```

- **The delimiter option**: This gives instructions to Stata regarding data insertion to `insheet`. Stata has the ability to recognize tab as well as comma-delimited data, yet often other delimiters such as `;` are used in datasets. Here is an example:

  ```
  insheet using "E:\Ind-samp.txt", delimiter (";")
  ```

Infix

Along with `insheet`, you can use the `infix` command, as shown later.

Most times, CSV or tab-delimited datasets are utilized, and the ASCII format is still used to save older data. Let's take the example of a survey taken by the government. This example represents two lines from 2010:

```
10862226023331    06 022  3  0222015550066660077700003331
10001222228332    06 022  3  0255555300666600000000044441
```

A codebook or data dictionary usually comes in the PDF or text file format. It explains the data that shows us that the first two numbers, the row ID, and the other two numericals are survey records (2010 from the previously mentioned dataset), and the fifth number is the quarter (the first quarter in this case) of the interview, among other things. `infix` is required to read such types of data and provides information to Stata from the codebook. The following is an example:

```
infix rowtype 1-2 yr 3-4 quart 5 […] using
"E:\ Stata1\Survey2010.dat", clear
```

In order to save many files, the `dictionary` file is used; it will save the codebook information and mark it as a separate file. The file can be seen as follows:

```
infix dictionary using Survey2010.dat
{
  dta
  rowtype   1-2
  yr   3-4 quart5 […]
}
```

The `infix` command is used after saving the data as `Survey2010.dct`. As a relative path is used in the dictionary file (`Survey2010`), it is believed that raw data will be inside the same file set that is either a dictionary or a catalogue file. This being the case, then referring data is not required. The file will look like this:

```
infix using "H:\ECStata\NHIS1986.dct", clear
```

Defining and constituting a dictionary file in a proper way is a tedious job. However, NHIS has a dictionary that can be read through the SAS program; this can be converted into Stata using the **Stat/Transfer** program.

The Stat/Transfer program

This program is used to convert various dataset formats into well-defined industry formats, such as SAS, R, SPSS, Excel, and so on. Before converting, the data should be examined thoroughly. As it is an extremely user-friendly tool, it can be used to change the data between various packages as well as formats. This is shown as follows:

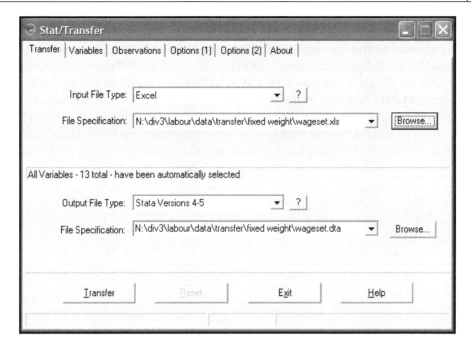

Manual typing or copy and paste

Typing or copying and pasting is the same as in other programs, but here, it can be done through the Stata editor. Just select the required data columns in Excel and paste them in the Stata editor. However, this has some drawbacks; many times, data inaccuracy or missing values don't have any fixed procedure, and in certain cases, language problems may arise. For example, in selected countries, a comma is used instead of a decimal point.

Typing is an extremely tough job, especially when electronic data is unavailable because in that case, we have to type the data. This job becomes easy in Stata through the `edit` command as it will take you to a spreadsheet-like feature where new data can be entered and old data can be edited.

Variables and data types

There are different types of variables and data types, which we are going to see in this section.

Indicators or data variables

To find the insights and the data conclusions, the browse/edit command is helpful. Data variables store the fundamental data. As shown in the following table, the income data for different nations is stored in the Cccgdp variable and the country (Countrycode) data is stored in the pop variable. If we want to get an idea about the details of all kinds of data, then one indicator variable is needed. In the following case, Countrycode and yr will provide information regarding the country, the year, the country's GDP, and the population data (pops). The data might be as follows:

Country	Countrycode	Yr	Pops	Cccgdp	Openss
India	IND	2010	23452.9	10897.23	23.11111
U.S.	USA	2010	22222.1	23987.23	90.42231
Pakistan	PAK	2010	11111.2	23675.21	10.22291
China	CHN	2010	98765	97654.94	30.98765
Russia	RUS	2010	19876	65745.11	43.34343
Germany	GER	2010	23467	23874.35	23.74747

After importing the data in Stata, it is always a good practice to examine the data. It gives you an advantage in any modeling or visualization exercise.

Examining the data

Examining the data is always recommended. It is a good idea to examine your data when you first read it into Stata; you should check whether all the variables and observations are present and are in the correct format.

While the browse/edit command is used to examine the raw data, the list command is used to see the results of the data. Listing small data is possible through this command. For bigger datasets, options are used to track the data. An example is shown as follows:

```
List country* yr pops

    Country        countrycode      yr        pops
    India          IND              2010      23452.9 |
    U.S.           USA              2010      22222.1 |
    Pakistan       PAK              2010      11111.2 |
    China          CHN              2010      98765 |
    Russia         RUS              2010      19876 |
    Germany        GER              2010      23467 |
```

In the preceding table, the star is called the **placeholder**, and it instructs Stata to incorporate the entire data with the country. Alternatively, we could focus on all variables but list only a limited number of observations, for example, the observation from 14th to 19th row:

The following table contains the country, country code, year, and pops 14/19:

Country	Countrycode	Yr	Popscon	Cccgdps	kOpenss
India	IND	2010	23452.9	10897.23	23.11111
U.S.	USA	2010	22222.1	23987.23	90.42231
Pakistan	PAK	2010	11111.2	23675.21	10.22291
China	CHN	2010	98765	97654.94	30.98765
Russia	RUS	2010	19876	65745.11	43.34343
Germany	GER	2010	23467	23874.35	23.74747

How to subset the data file using IN and IF

In the previous part, the `in` qualifier was used; it makes sure that the subset pertains to selected data. A lot of observations follow after this, for example:

- The list in 14/19
- The list in 90/1
- The list in 30/1

As is clear from the preceding example, there are three observations:

- The first command lists observations from 14 to 19
- The second command lists 90 observations
- The third command lists observations from 30 till the last observation

The `if` statement is the other way of subsetting data; it generally has values of *true* or *false*. The following is an example from the observation of the year 2010, where the variable name is *yr*:

```
list if yr == 2010
```

In order to examine the raw data, the `browse` window is used. However, a problem occurs when only selected variables are to be viewed; this happens in big datasets. So, in this condition, create a list of the variables you want to examine before browsing. This is done through the following command:

```
browse country yr popscon
```

It is important to note that this `edit` command will help change the dataset manually. The `assert` command helps Stata examine the observation. This is because when the bigger data (or big data, as it is called in today's world) arrives, checking single data through `browse` or `edit` commands becomes difficult. In this case, the `assert` command is helpful. There are a couple of advantages: it helps identify whether a data statement is right or wrong. For example, in the case of the population of the country (`popscon`), it will tell us that the values are positive:

```
assert popscon>0,

assert popscon<0
```

If the preceding command results in the value *true*, then `assert` does not give any output. However, if the command value is *false*, then an error message will appear.

The `describe` command accounts for various fundamental information regarding datasets and variables, such as the total size of the dataset and the variable, the total number of variables in the dataset, and different formats of the variables. This can be denominated as `describe`. It can only be applied to an unread file in Stata. An example is given as follows:

```
describe using "E:\Ind-Health-sample.dta"
```

Codebook can give information on variables in the dataset without the list of variables; an example of this is codebook country.

The `summarize` command delivers the statistics summary: means, standard deviation, and so on. The following table represents this tab:

```
summarize table
```

Variable	Obs	Mean	Std. Dev.	Min	Max
Cntry	0				
countrycode	0				
Yr	97	2000	2.156	1990	2010
Popscon	97	87634.46	8374.33	29383.9	93830
ccCgdps	97	67544.23	4100.682	15890.71	98739.67
kOpenss	97	34	4	13	50
Chi-ppl	97	23.6	3.56	10.456	40.8796
Fdhsa	97	19.56	9.567	12.456	34.98765
Gdkliyu	97	1.987456	1.2	-3.238917	6.46896

As we can see in the preceding table, string variables such as `Cntry` and `Countrycode` do not have numbers; this is why no summary details are available. `Yr` is a numeric variable; therefore, we can see that it has a statistics summary. For more details, the summarize detail option can be used.

The wide range of graphic qualities makes Stata a unique tool. One can easily get help by typing the `help` command in Stata. A histogram graph can be created through the following command:

```
graph twoway histogram cccgdps
```

For a scatter plot, you have to leverage the following command:

```
graph two-way scatter ccccgdps popscon
```

Even though there is some benefit of having advanced graphs in Stata, this makes it work slowly. In certain cases, it is better to use version 7 graphics because they help visualize the data properly without using papers or presentations. This can be seen as follows:

```
graph7 cccgdps popscon
```

Saving the dataset is a very easy command, and it is represented as follows:

```
Save "E:\Stata1\t1 less India pwt 80-2010.dta", replace
```

If we have sets of files of the same content, then the `replace` tab/option can be helpful. It will swap the last version and save it. If the old version is to be stored for some reason, then save it with a different name. One thing that should be kept in mind is that the original file content can be changed if it is saved with revised datasets. Therefore, after changes are made to the revised file, in order to open the file and restart it, just reopen it.

There are two ways to preserve and store the data. One option is to save the current data and revise it, and later, if you don't want to keep the data, then `reopen` the saved data version. Another option is to use the `preserve` and `restore` functions/commands; they will take an image of the data, and the data will come back after you type `restore`.

Summary

We discussed lots of basic commands, which can be leveraged while performing Stata programming. The next chapter will discuss data management techniques and programming in detail. This chapter is basic and will help any beginner-level Stata programmer start working on Stata.

As you learn more about Stata, you will understand the various commands and functions and their business applications.

2
Stata Programming and Data Management

This chapter will showcase the labeling methodology of the variables in Stata. It is really important to understand the data management aspects of Stata, which are covered in depth in this chapter. We will cover the following topics:

- The labeling of the data, variables, and variable transformations
- Summarizing the data and preparing tabulated reports
- Appending and merging the files for data management

The labeling of data, variables, and variable transformations

Stata is easy to use and gives you the leverage point of labeling different variables in the data you have acquired/imported. It also allows you to:

- Label the dataset itself
- Label different value signs in the imported dataset
- Label various variables in the imported dataset

For example, let's assume that we have a dataset with no labels. The name of the dataset/filename is `Fridge_sales`.

You can leverage Stata functions and commands and do not have to write code from the beginning.

To get details of the current dataset (`Fridge_sales`), type the following command in Stata:

describe

Here is the output of this command:

```
Contains data from Fridge_sales
Obs              30                          2000 Fridge sales data
vars             10                          17 Jun 2015 10:12
size          2,000 (80% of memory free)     (_dta has notes)
-------------------------------------------------------------------------------
        variable name    storage type  display format    value label    variable  label
model          str18       %-18s
cost           int         %8.0gc
weight         int         %8.0gc
volume         int         %8.0gc
door length    int         %8.0gc
door width     int         %8.0gc
door type      int         %8.0gc
temp ratio     int         %8.0gc
complaints     str18       %-18s
-------------------------------------------------------------------------------
Sorted by:
```

Now, you can leverage a command called `label data` so that you can add the label that can describe the dataset in detail. The label of the dataset can have a maximum length of *80* characters. To label the data, use the following command:

label data "This dataset has fridge sales data from year 2000"

As discussed previously in the `describe` command, the label is applied to the dataset, as shown in the following screenshot:

```
Contains data from Fridge_sales
Obs              30                                This dataset has fridge sales data from year 2000
vars             10                                17 Jun 2015 10:12
size          2,000 (80% of memory free)           (_dta has notes)

--------------------------------------------------------------------------------------------------
          variable name    storage type  display format     value label      variable  label
model            str18       %-18s
cost             int         %8.0gc
weight           int         %8.0gc
volume           int         %8.0gc
door length      int         %8.0gc
door width       int         %8.0gc
door type        int         %8.0gc
temp ratio       int         %8.0gc
complaints       str18       %-18s
--------------------------------------------------------------------------------------------------
Sorted by:
```

You can utilize the `label variable` command, which can label different variables in the dataset:

```
label variable model    "model numbers of the fridges dispatched in year
2000"
label variable cost    "the cost of the fridge in 2000"
label variable weight    "weight of the fridge dispatched in 2000"
label variable volume "volume of the fridge dispatched in 2000"
```

Apply the `describe` command to the dataset so that you can view the changes:

```
Contains data from Fridge_sales
Obs              30                     This dataset has fridge sales data from year 2000
vars             10                     17 Jun 2015 10:12
size          2,000 (80% of memory free)  (_dta has notes)
--------------------------------------------------------------------------------
          variable name   storage type  display format   value label   variable  label
model           str18        %-18s                                      model numbers of the fridges dispatched in year 2000
cost            int          %8.0gc                                     the cost of the fridge in 2000
weight          int          %8.0gc                                     weight of the fridge dispatched in 2000
volume          int          %8.0gc                                     volume of the fridge dispatched in 2000
door length     int          %8.0gc
door width      int          %8.0gc
door type       int          %8.0gc
temp ratio      int          %8.0gc
complaints      str18        %-18s
--------------------------------------------------------------------------------
Sorted by:
```

Summarizing the data and preparing tabulated reports

Now, we will use the `Fridge_sales` data for further commands. For this, you need to inform Stata that you will be using `Fridge_sales_data` with the following command:

```
use fridge_sales_data
```

Now, in this data, the variables' volume denotes the volume of the fridge. How do you generate this variable in Stata? Your answer lies in using the `summarize` command:

```
summarize volume
```

The output of this command is as follows:

Variable	Obs	Mean	Std. Dev.	Min	Max
volume	30	124.2	12	100	150

Now, you need to create a new variable called `volume_ratio`. The `volume` ratio denotes the fridge volume divided by 20:

```
generate volume_ratio = volume / 20
```

The `generate` command creates new variables in the given dataset. Similarly, for existing variables that need to be treated and made perfect for further analysis, you can use the `replace` command:

For example, take a look at the following:

```
replace volume = volume / 20
```

Now, you can see the changes between the original variable and the derived variable using the `summarize` command:

```
summarize volume volume_ratio
```

Here are the results of the summarize command:

Variable	Obs	Mean	Std. Dev.	Min	Max
volume	30	124.2	12	100	150
Volume_ratio	30	6	2	2	7

Now, let's discuss the syntax behind both the commands, `generate` and `replace`. Superficially, they look as if they are twin brothers. However, they have some differences. The `generate` command will work only if the variable is not available in the dataset. `replace` works well when the variable is available in the dataset and you need to transform that variable into a better form in order to conduct further modeling activities. If the variable is not available and you use the `replace` command, then it shows an error.

For example, you need to generate a new variable that is the cube of the volume values. Here is how you do this:

```
generate volume3 = volume^3
summarize volume3
```

The output of this command is as follows:

Variable	Obs	Mean	Std. Dev.	Min	Max
volume3	30	1000023	384	1000000	2100000

What if you need to see which values are present in the dataset for a given variable? For this, you can use the `tabulate` command:

```
tabulate volume
```

The output of this command is as follows:

Volume	Freq	Percent	Cum.
100	2	6.67	6.67
105	2	6.67	13.33
110	2	6.67	20.00
115	2	6.67	26.67
117	2	6.67	33.33
118	2	6.67	40.00
120	1	3.33	43.33
121	1	3.33	46.67
122	1	3.33	50.00
123	2	6.67	56.67
124	2	6.67	63.33
125	6	20.00	83.33
130	1	3.33	86.67
135	1	3.33	90.00
140	1	3.33	93.33
145	1	3.33	96.67
150	1	3.33	100.00
Total	30	100.00	

What happens when you convert the volume by applying conditions to the variable? For example, look at the following:

```
generate volume3    = .
 (12 missing values generated)
replace   volume3   = 11 if (volume <= 110)
(17 real changes made)
replace   volume3   = 22 if (mpg >= 110) & (mpg <=130)
 (11 real changes made)
replace   volume3   = 3 if (mpg >= 130) & (mpg <.)
Keep:
```

Many times, you do not need all the variables in the dataset. Let's take the example of the `Fridge_sales` data that we discussed previously. Here is snapshot of the overall dataset:

```
describe
```

The output of this command is as follows:

```
Contains data from Fridge_sales
Obs              30                      2000 Fridge sales data
vars             10                      17 Jun 2015 10:12
size             2,000 (80% of memory free)   (_dta has notes)

--------------------------------------------------------------------------------
         variable name      storage type  display format   value label    variable  label
model          str18        %-18s
cost           int          %8.0gc
weight         int          %8.0gc
volume         int          %8.0gc
door length    int          %8.0gc
door width     int          %8.0gc
door type      int          %8.0gc
temp ratio     int          %8.0gc
complaints     str18        %-18s
--------------------------------------------------------------------------------
Sorted by:
```

Now, you may want to keep only the first three variables, that is, `model`, `cost`, and `weight`. Here is the code to perform this activity:

```
keep model cost weight
describe
```

```
Contains data from Fridge_sales
Obs              30              This dataset has fridge sales data from year 2000
vars             10              17 Jun 2015 10:12
size             2,000 (80% of memory free)   (_dta has notes)

--------------------------------------------------------------------------------
         variable name      storage ty display fo value label variable   label
model          str18        %-18s                       model numbers of the fridges dispatched in year 2000
cost           int          %8.0gc                      the cost of the fridge in 2000
weight         int          %8.0gc                      weight of the fridge dispatched in 2000
--------------------------------------------------------------------------------
Sorted by:
```

What if you need to drop a few variables and keep the rest of them as is? The answer lies in the drop command. Here is how you can utilize the drop command:

```
drop model cost weight
describe
```

The output of this command is as follows:

```
Contains data from Fridge_sales
Obs              30                  This dataset has fridge sales data from year 2000
vars             10                  17 Jun 2015 10:12
size             2,000 (80% of memory free)   (_dta has notes)

------------------------------------------------------------------
        variable name    storage ty display fo value label variable   label
volume          int      %8.0gc                               volume of the fridge dispatched in 2000
door length     int      %8.0gc
door width      int      %8.0gc
door type       int      %8.0gc
temp ratio      int      %8.0gc
complaints      str18    %-18s
------------------------------------------------------------------
Sorted by:
```

Now, you need to have summarized versions in order to showcase these dataset insights to the higher management, such as the average of the volume, cost, and sales.

Here is how you achieve this:

```
collapse cost
list
```

Here is the result:

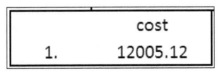

	cost
1.	12005.12

This shows you the average of the costs of all the fridges that were sold in year 2000. What if you need the average of costs by `model`? Here is the Stata code for this:

```
collapse cost, by(model)
list
collapse (mean) average=cost, by(model)
list
```

Here are the results:

	model	Average
1.	model 1	11245.02
2.	model 2	12001.03
3.	model3	13812.92

```
collapse (mean) avgcost=age avgvolume=volume, by(model)
list
```

	model	Avgcost	Avgvolume
1.	model 1	11245.02	110
2.	model 2	12001.03	125
3.	model3	13812.92	145

Appending and merging the files for data management

Now, let's discuss how to work with more than one file. We will create two data files and combine them in different ways.

Let's create the first data file in Stata:

```
input fridge_model_id str10 model cost
1 "model 1" 12000
2 "model 2" 20000
3 "model 3" 40000
End
Save fridge_model, replace
List
```

	fridge_model_id	model	cost
1.	1	model 1	12000
2.	2	model 2	20000
3.	3	model 3	40000

Let's create the second dataset:

```
Clear
Input fridge_model_id str10 model cost
1 "model 4" 42000
2 "model 5" 52000
3 "model 6" 62000
End
Save fridge_model2, replace
List
```

	fridge_model_id	model	cost
4.	4	model 4	42000
5.	5	model 5	52000
6.	6	model 6	62000

Now, let's append the two files we created:

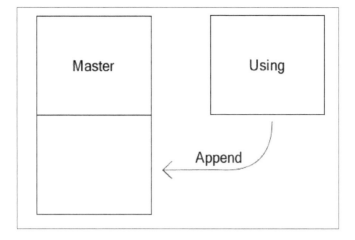

```
use fridge_model, clear
append using fridge_model2
```

	fridge_model_id	model	cost
1.	1	model 1	12000
2.	2	model 2	20000
3.	3	model 3	40000
4.	4	model 4	42000
5.	5	model 5	52000
6.	6	model 6	62000

Now, let's take the **fridge_model** data that has been prepared and sort it by **fridge_model_id**:

```
use fridge_model, clear
sort fridge_model _id
save fridge_model3
list
```

	fridge_model_id	model	cost
1.	1	model 1	12000
2.	2	model 2	20000
3.	3	model 3	40000

Let's create the second dataset for these models:

```
clear
input fridge_model_id str10 length width
1 100 200
2 150 300
3 200 400
end

sort fridge_model_id

save fridge_extra

list
```

	fridge_model_id	length	width
1.	1	100	200
2.	2	150	300
3.	3	200	400

Now, let's merge two files together on the basis of the variable that is sorted. In this case, `fridge_model_id` is used to sort both the files, and it is a common variable as well.

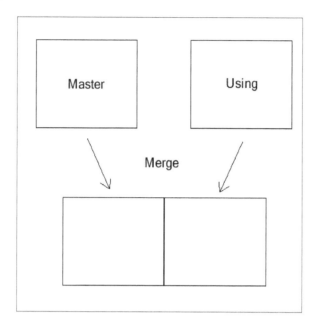

```
use fridge_model3, clear
merge famid using fridge_extra
```

```
list fridge_model_id model cost length width
```

	fridge_model_id	model	cost	length	width
1.	1	model 1	12000	100	200
2.	2	model 2	20000	150	300
3.	3	model 3	40000	200	400

Macros

A Stata macro is not a black box where we can input the text and numbers. You can use this module or box in various commands. One of the best tricks in Stata is to leverage many macro statements or, as they are rightly called, modules or boxes in a single Stata command and optimize the entire code.

First, let's look at local macros. If you are an experienced programmer, you might know the difference between global variables and local variables. This difference remains in Stata as well. Most of the macros in Stata are local macros and are written for specific commands or functions that can be reused for many occasions.

For example, take a look at the following command:

```
local macro_Name table
```

For example:

```
local Y 9
```

In this command or macro, the name of the macro is Y and 9 is the denotation of the table. Another example can be as follows:

```
display "Y"
```

On a general note, all the macros are processed by the macro processor. The macro processor properly feeds the macros to Stata. When Stata recognizes the macro along with questions marks, it replaces the variables and table names with its variables and the tables available from the data. For example, look at the following:

```
display 9
```

We can try out a bit more complex macro now:

```
local Y 9+9
display 'Y'
```

Obviously, the outcome of the query or the macro is 18. The display program is almost a calculator in this case. The Stata program for a similar macro would have been as follows:

```
display 9+9
```

Every time you need to 9+9, you will have to write this entire command, which can be avoided by writing just a small macro.

What if you need to save the results or the outcome of the Stata program in the given Stata macro? You can leverage the variables in which you save the macro results or outcomes on various occasions while executing the Stata coding.

For example, look at the following:

```
local Y = 9+9
display "Y"
```

The saving or storing of the results happens through the equals (=) sign and can be leveraged in the lot of ways. In this case, Y stores the digit 18 as a result of the calculation that was performed, that is, 9 + 9. This value of Y can be utilized on multiple occasions, wherever you need to insert in the code, rather than writing the entire code.

For macro-related expressions you can use the following syntax:

```
'=expression'
```

The expression command is the equation, the formula, or the calculation that needs to be evaluated. For example, look at the following:

```
display "'=9+9'"
```

The outcome of the query is 18. However, display does not calculate this outcome. The equals sign after the double inverted comma suggests that the Stata macro process needs to calculate what comes after the sign. The other way in which you can use this is as follows:

```
'=dis_N'
```

This denotes the total number of observations in the current data file or dataset in use. Now, let's move to the part that talks about embedding one macro in the other. This part is the most useful one in the entire Stata programming process, where you can keep on embedding multiple macros into a single macro, which can act as a single piece of code and get done with various things.

For example:

```
display '='Y' - 9'
```

This tells the processor to reduce the value of Y by 9, and the value of Y comes through the previous macro. Now, Stata's biggest problem is that it does not give you the error message when the macro you want to run is not defined.

Stata's macro process takes this as nothing and displays nothing. For example, look at the following:

```
display 'z'
```

If you ever mistype the name of the macro or type the wrong spelling of the macro, it does not give you an error message. This can be extremely tough to find if your programs are larger than normal length. Due to this reason, you need to be really careful while using macros.

Loops in Stata

Loops is a very important concept in Stata. For various calculations and executions, putting code into loops is an extremely useful concept. The command used to create loops in Stata is `foreach`. The syntax for such a command is as follows:

```
foreach macro_name in list_name {
command(s)
}
```

Now, let's take a small example:

```
Foreach ball_size in ten twenty thirty [
display " 'ball_size' "
]
```

In this code, `ball_size` acts as the name of the written macro. It has a list of the elements that need to be part of the macro. Stata's macro processor breaks this list into appropriate sections. In this case, the sections of the current code can be as per the element list, such as ten, twenty, and thirty.

The brackets denote the beginning and the ending of the loop:

- `[`: This denotes the beginning of the loop
- `]`: This denotes the end of the loop

The Stata macro processor analyzes the entire list, which is your input in the macro statement. It also identifies all the elements in the list. For the first element, Stata prints ten; for the second, it prints twenty, and so on. The loop goes on until the list of elements is exhausted.

You can also write a loop where you involve lots of variables as a part of the loop. Now, you can run the regression in a loop with all the variables that can be dependent and independent variables.

```
Foreach ball_size in ten twenty thrity [
Reg 'ball_size' color weight
]
```

You can also rename the variables in the loop for which you might have to write a big program otherwise. For example, look at the following:

```
Foreach ball_size of varlist * [
local new_name = lower (" 'old_name' ")
Rename 'old_name' 'new_name'
]
```

You can also write a loop irrespective of the variable values that run for a definite amount of loops. For example, look at the following:

```
Forvalues j = 1/20 [
display 'j'
]
```

This query will give you the following result:

```
1
2
3
4
5
6
7
8
9
10
11
12
13
14
15
16
17
18
19
20
```

Another example can be finding out the year in which China's GDP was more than 8. 1 indicates a GDP more than 8, and less than 1 indicates a GDP of less than 8:

```
Forvalues year = 2001/2015 {
Gen with 'year' = (gdp'year' > 1) if gdp'year' <1
}
```

This will produce the following outcome:

```
2001
2002
2003
2005
2007
2009
2010
2012
2013
```

Now, let's move on to the loop nesting part where we can have more than one loop embedded in each other. For example, look at the following:

```
Forval a = 1/5 {
Forval b = 1/5 {
display " 'a' 'b' "
}
}
```

This creates the following result:

```
1,1
1,2
1,3
1,4
1,5
2,1
2,2
2,3
2,4
2,5
3,1
3,2
3,3
3,4
3,5
4,1
4,2
4,3
4,4
4,5
5,1
5,2
5,3
5,4
5,5
```

While loops

While loops are similar to for loops and work in various ways in Stata. Here is an example of a `while` loop:

```
local a 1
while 'a' <= 15 {
display 'a++'}
```

Another example is as follows:

```
local a 1
While 'a' <= 15
{
display 'a' = 'a'+1
}
```

This has the following values as a part of the output:

```
1
2
3
4
5
6
7
8
9
10
11
12
13
14
15
```

The equivalent `for` loop for this query is as follows:

```
Forval a = 1/15 {
display 'a'}
```

In the following few chapters, we will learn how to perform graphing operations and statistical modeling in Stata. It is extremely useful to learn these macros, loops, and programming in Stata well in order to understand the next few chapters well.

Generally, all the variables defined in Stata are vectors. These variables can have multiple values. When you use the `display` command in such vector cases, you get the first value of the variable. For example, look at the following:

```
display a
```

This will give you the output that is the first value of a. If you need a specific value of the vector, then you have to define that as a part of the array. For example, look at the following:

```
display a[20]
```

This code will give you the 20th value of the vector a.

Summary

In this chapter, we learned how to manage data by changing labels, how to create new variables, and how to replace the existing variables and make them better from a modeling perspective. We also learned how to drop and keep the important variables for analysis, how to summarize the data tables into report formats, and how to append or merge different data files.

In one sentence, you learned how to prepare reports and prepare the data for further graphs and modeling assignments.

In the next chapter, we will talk about the graphical interpretation of the data and the visualization of the data for a better understanding of the data you are handling.

3

Data Visualization

Stata graphics is one of the most important parts that we need to know before we start with modeling. Till now, we have covered basic Stata programs, macros, and data management knowledge and application. This chapter will showcase how to develop different graphs and visualizations in Stata.

Here are some of the topics that we will cover in this chapter:

- Scatter plots
- Line graphs
- Histogram/bar charts and other graphs
- Statistical calculations in graphs
- Curve fitting in Stata graphs

Scatter plots

Let's start with scatter plots. Assume that your data has variable A and variable B with a lot of values. You need to find a correlation between variable A and variable B. Before you find the correlation, you need to plot the scatter graph of these two variables.

Select **twoway** graphs from the Stata tool list and follow the following steps:

1. Click on the **Create** button. Here is what the box will look like:

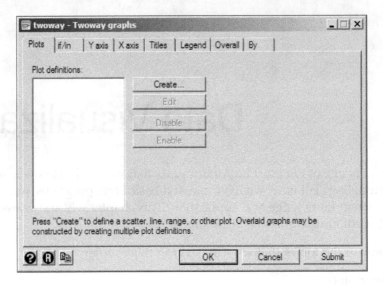

2. Select **Basic plots** and select the type of the plot as **Scatter** plot.

3. Select **X** and **Y** variable, as shown in the next screenshot:

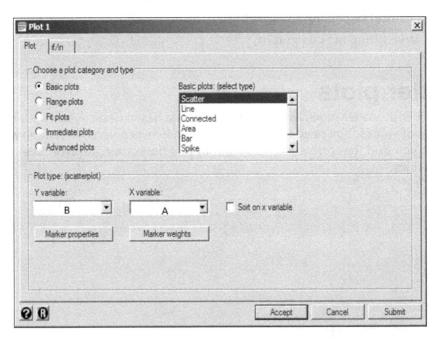

4. Click on the **Accept** button after performing the required changes, as shown in the preceding screenshot.

5. Your output window will open with scatter plot, as shown in the next screenshot:

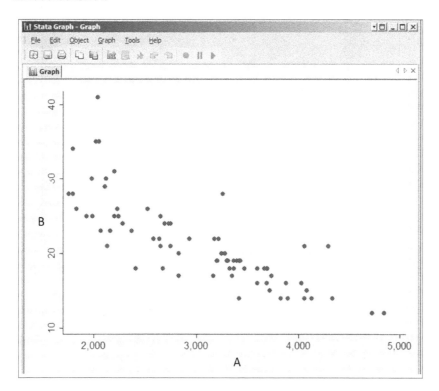

What if you need to add more variables and create complex scatter plots? You can add as many variables as you want and observe the clusters that are naturally available in the scatter plot. Here is a procedure to perform this:

1. Click on the **graphing** tool again.

2. In the list of variables that acted as an input for **Y** axis variable, type variable **C**.

3. **C** is the new variable that you need to upload on the scatter plot along with variable **B**.

4. The **X** axis will have the same variable as **A**.

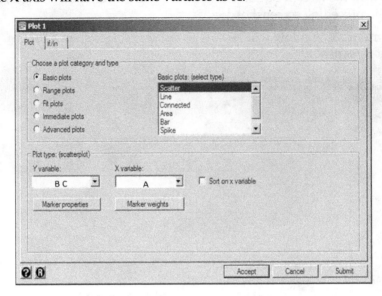

This will tell the Stata processor that there are two variables that need to be inserted from the **Y** axis and plotted against variable **A**, which is the input for the **X** axis.

5. When you click on **Accept**, you will get the following scatter plot:

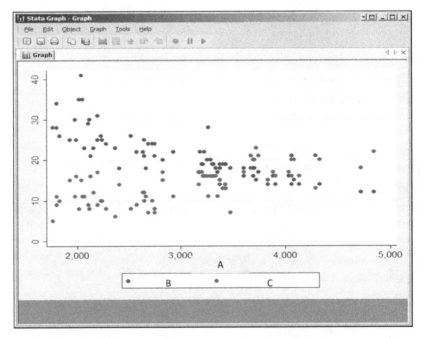

Scatter plots are extremely useful in identifying the following, which naturally exist in the dataset used for analysis:

- Correlations
- Clusters

What if you need to plot a subset of the variable depending on a certain condition? Take a look at the following steps:

1. Press tab and click on **if/in**.
2. Type **Include** in **if** box.
3. This will include the data points where the flag of the row is equal to **include**.

    Here is how you perform the preceding activity:

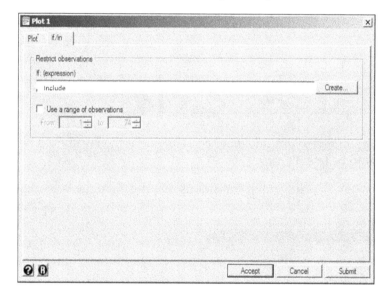

4. Once you put the condition of **Include** in the box, click on the **Accept** button. Here is the output of the query:

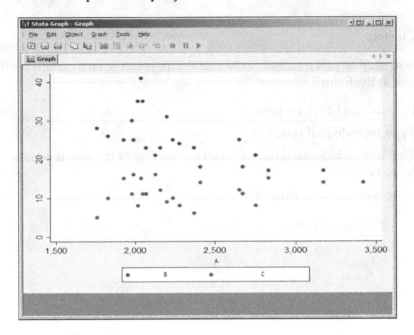

5. Now, you need to put one more condition that the tag should be **include** and **D** should be less than *10*.

    Here is how you insert the conditions into the dialogue box opened after clicking on the **if/in** button:

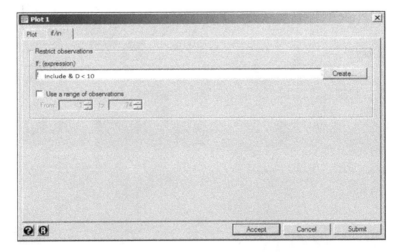

This is what the output looks like:

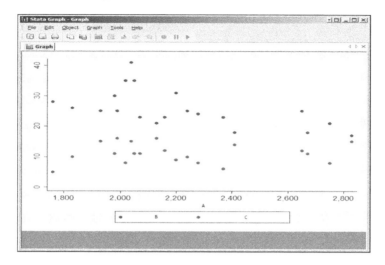

Line plots

Line plots follow a methodology similar to that of scatter plots. The difference is that you need to select the **Line** type of graph from the window shown in the following screenshot:

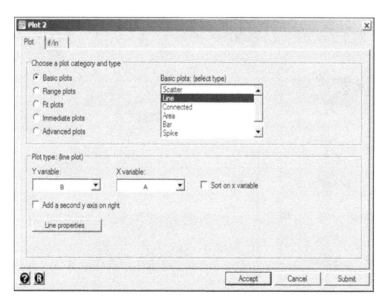

The output is shown as follows:

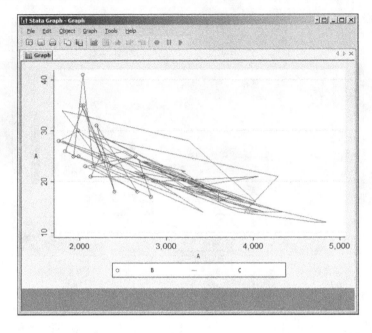

You can also sort the graph on the variable that is input to the **X** axis. The procedure to sort the graph by the **X** axis variable in order to find better patterns is shown as follows:

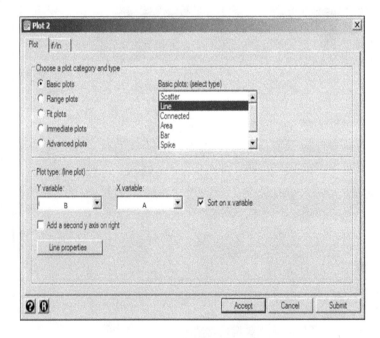

Here is the output, which looks drastically different from the first graph and shows you completely different patterns:

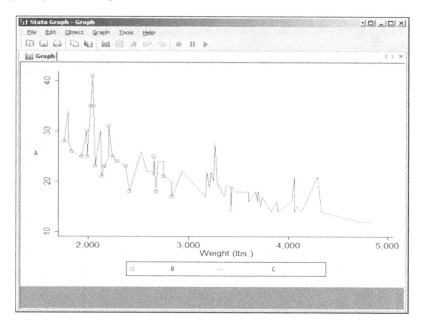

You can also change the line properties of the line graph shown in the preceding screenshot:

1. Click on **Line properties** and select the **Pattern** option.
2. Select **Dash** from the list of drop-down options for the pattern box.

   Here are a few screenshots that show you how to perform this operation:

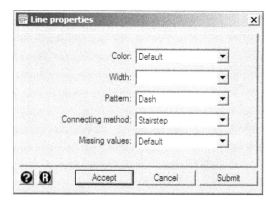

Here is how the graph is prepared:

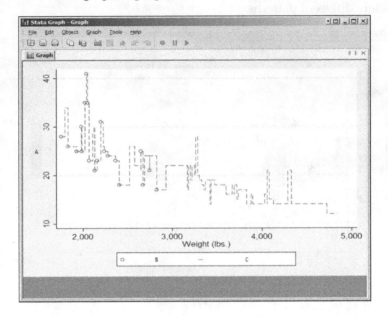

Histograms and other charts

Stata creates a lot of histograms as well. You can also create graphs by writing code instead of using Stata frontend/GUI; for example, take a look at the following:

```
two-way bar A B
```

The output of this command is shown in the following figure:

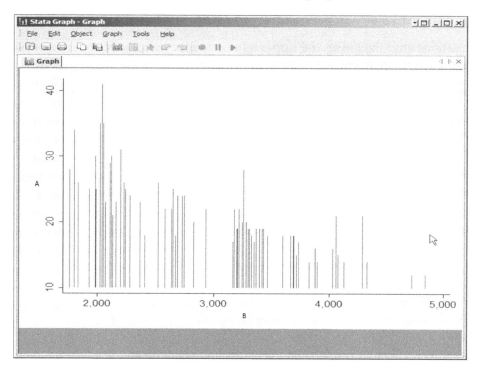

Box plots

Another way to look at data is box plots; they are also called **box and whiskers** plots.

In box plots, a box ranges from a quartile in the lower range, which is also 25th percentile of data, to a quartile in the upper range, which is the 75th percentile. It also contains a line in the median value, which is the 50th percentile.

Then, you have whiskers plots. Whiskers generally range from the quartile with a low value and a low adjacent value to the quartile in the upper range and upper adjacent value.

Lower Adjacent Value = lower quartile − 3/ 2 IQR

Upper Adjacent Value = upper quartile + 3/2 IQR

Observations after the lower and upper adjacent value are plotted in terms of points; for example, take a look at the following:

```
graph box scores
```

The output of this command is shown in the following figure:

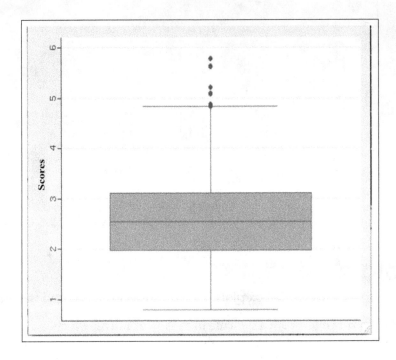

You can divide these graphs by categorical variables; for example, take a look at the following:

```
-graph box scores, over(sex)
```

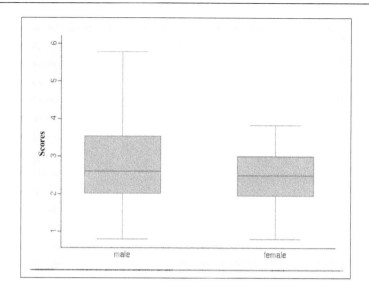

Pie charts

You can look at the given data in terms of pie charts as well. Pie charts are generally good for business presentations, showing the market share, and so on.

In this example, we will show you the disease prevalence of the New York state:

```
graph pie hospital_admission, over(disease) sort descending
```

The output of this is shown in the following figure:

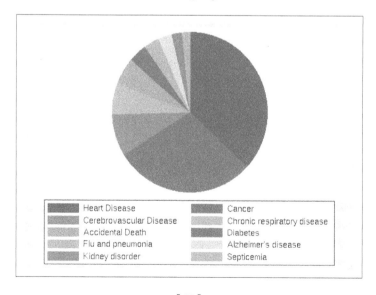

Pyramidal graphs

What if we need a pyramidal graph divided into all possible subcategories of the data? Here is your answer in terms of the Stata code:

```
egen scoregroup= cut(score), group(9) label
tab scoregroup

sort sex scoregroup session
contract sex scoregroup session
rename _freq cnt

reshape wide cnt, i(scoregroup sex) j(session)

gen d1 = cnt1 /*session = 1 */
gen d12 = cnt1+cnt2
gen d123 = cnt3 + d12
gen d1_n = - d1
gen d12_n = - d12
gen d123_n = - d123


gen zero = 0

label values scoregroup scoregroup
label values sex f1

twoway bar c123 scoregroup if sex==0 , horizontal || ///
  bar c12 scoregroup if sex==0, horizontal || ///
  bar c1 scoregroup if sex ==0, horizontal   || ///
  bar c123_n scoregroup if sex ==1 , horizontal || ///
  bar c12_n scoregroup if sex ==1, horizontal || ///
  bar c1_n scoregroup if sex ==1, horizontal || ///

  sc  scoregroup zero ,  mlabel(scoregroup) mlabsize(vsmall) ///
  mlabcolor(white) msymbol(i) || , plotregion(style(none)) ysca(dash)
  ///
```

```
ylabel(none) xsca(dash titlegap(-1)) xlabel(0 -30 "30" -20 "20" ///
10(10) 20 , tlength(0) labsize(vsmall) grid gmin gmax) ytitle(score
groups) ///
legend(order(- "Female" - "Male" 5 2 6  3 7 4) col(3) lab(2 "high
session") ///
lab(3 "med session") lab(4 "low session") lab(5 "high session")
lab(6 "med session") ///
lab(7 "low session") lab(8 " ") colgap(59) symysize(1) size(vsmall)
bmargin(small) rowgap(*.5))
```

In this case, you will get the following graph:

Vio plots

You can also use different techniques, such as vio plots. For example, in the case of scores given to people who give interviews in a company for a job, for different traits, you can plot the distribution in a much better way in order to understand how everyone population who is giving the interview is performing. Take a look at the following code snippet:

```
vioplot domain_knowledge attitude aptitude personality, hor
```

The `vioplot` command is a user-defined command, and you can write your own commands, which we can leverage. The output of this command will look like the following graph:

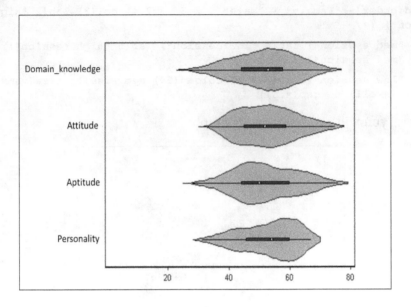

Ci plots

Ci plots is user-defined command. You can also try `ciplots`. The command for this is as follows:

```
ciplot domain_knowledge attitude aptitude personality, hor
```

The output of this command will looks like a following graph:

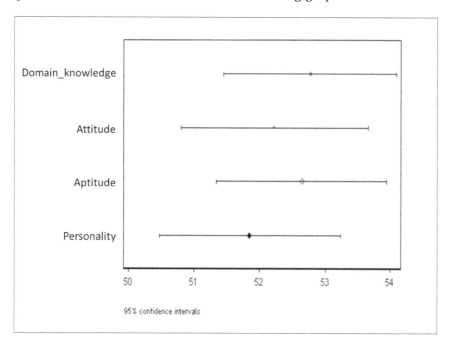

Statistical calculations in graphs

The command for statistical calculations in graphs is as follows:

```
Graph bar A B, over (Tag)
```

The result of this command will look like a following graph:

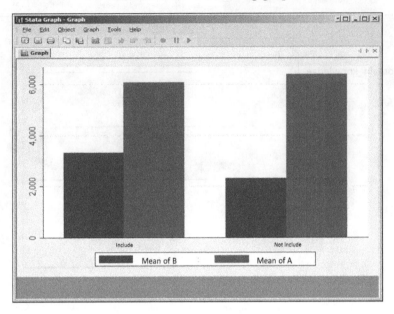

The command for this is as follows:

```
graph hbar A B, over(tag)
```

The output of this command will look like a following graph:

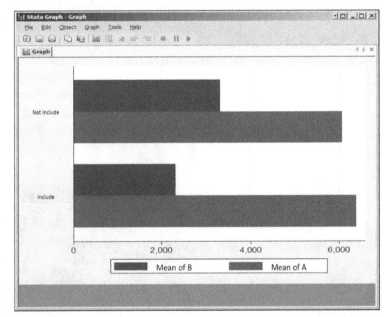

You can also perform median-related calculations and plot the medians accordingly. Here is the code to achieve this:

```
graph hbar (median) A B, over(Tag)
```

The following is the output you get after performing median calculations:

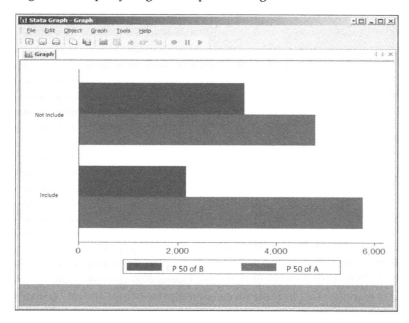

We can perform and create the independent kernel density plot by leveraging the `kdensity` code:

```
kdensity A
```

The output of this command will look like the following graph:

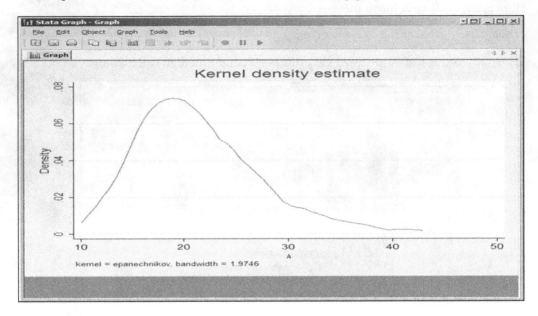

Kernel density estimation, which is also known as **KDE**, is a nonparametric tool that's used to plot the graphs of a selected variable. This is also part of a data-smoothing exercise and is heavily used in economics, signal processing, and the **consumer packaged goods** (CPG) industry in order to find various patterns of density.

You can also change the bandwidth of the data instead of the default bandwidth that was used in an earlier example. Here is the code for this:

```
kdensity A, bwidth(5)
```

The output of this command will look like the following graph:

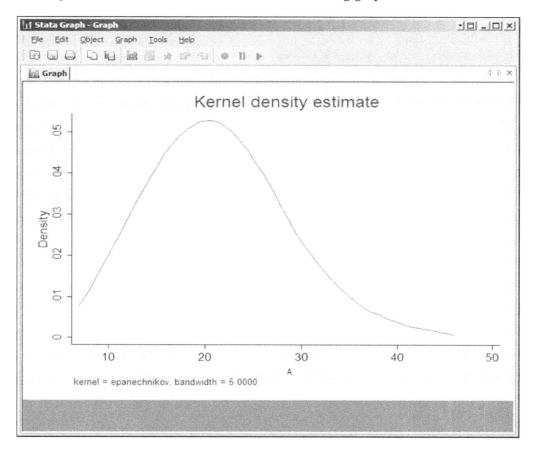

You can also leverage the graph editor to change anything in the graph that you have created:

1. Click on **File.**
2. Click on **Graph editor**.

    This is what the graph editor looks like:

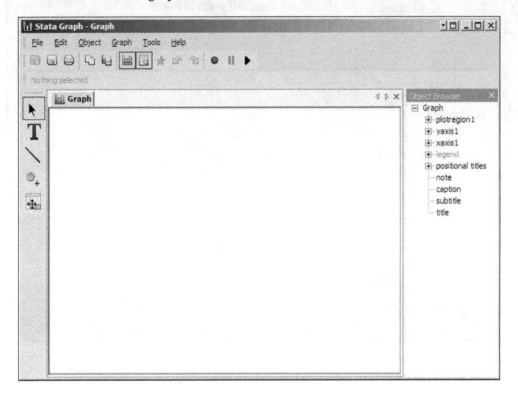

You can also change the axis properties by clicking on **Axis properties**, as shown in the following screenshot:

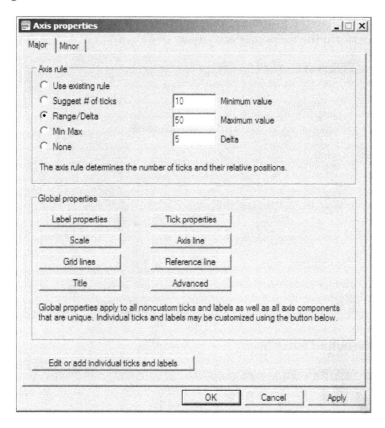

Curve fitting in Stata

You can also run regression/curve fitting or basic predictive analytics using graphs.
You need to go back to the graphing tool, as discussed in the beginning of the
chapter, and perform the following activities:

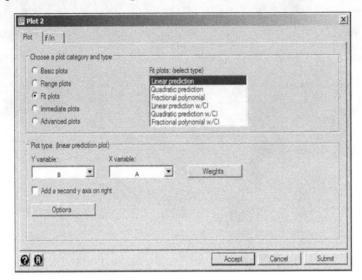

This is what the output looks like:

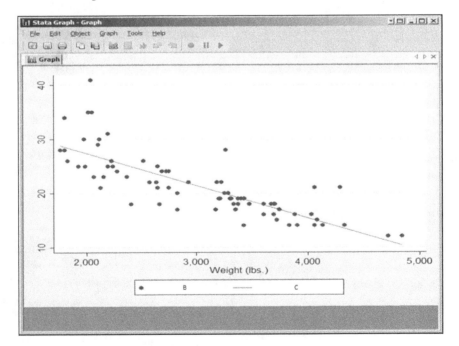

Summary

In this chapter, we discussed scatter plots, histograms, and various graphing techniques and the nitty-gritty involved in the visualization of the data in Stata. This chapter showcased how to perform visualization in Stata through code and graphical interfaces. Both are equally effective ways of creating graphs and visualizations.

Stata also helps you create predictive models and good fit / curve fitting in graphs. We showed you an example of this toward the end of the chapter. The next chapter onward, we will concentrate on the predictive modeling and data analytics part of Stata.

4
Important Statistical Tests in Stata

Before you start with modeling in Stata, you need to check distributions of data and conduct some statistical tests on the data. There are various tests that you need in order to conduct and perform operations as far as data distributions are concerned; this will help you understand the data better and create better models.

Here are some of the topics that we will cover in this chapter:

- T tests
- The chi-square test
- ANOVA
- MANOVA
- Fisher's exact test
- The Wilcoxon-Mann-Whitney test

T tests

Let's start with t tests. A sample t test gives you a leverage point to check whether the sample mean that can have a normally distributed variable has a significant difference from the hypothesis value. For example, you need to test whether the fridge sales average is significantly different from 10000. Here is the command to run the t test:

```
ttest fridge_sales = 10000
```

This command checks whether the mean or average of `fridge_sales` differs significantly from `10000`. Here is the exact formula for a sample t test:

$$t = \frac{\overline{x} - \mu_0}{s/\sqrt{n}}$$

Here are the results of **One-sample t test** as per the command that's run in Stata:

One-sample t test

Variable	Obs	Mean	Std. Err.	Std. Dev.	[95% Conf. Interval]	
write	100	9700	0.754	7.456	9634	9823

Degrees of freedom: 99

Ho: mean(fridge_sales) = 10000

Ha: mean < 10000	Ha: mean ~=10000	Ha: mean > 10000
t = 4.1405	t = 4.1405	t = 4.1405
P < t = 1.0000	P > |t| = 0.0001	P > t = 0.0000

This result shows that there is a statistically significant difference between the mean values of **fridge_sales** and **10000**. Let's see whether you have more than one group to compare the means. In this case, you can use two independent sample t-tests.

Two independent sample t tests

Independent samples' t tests are utilized when we need to compare and check the averages of a variable that is normally distributed and the interval dependent on two mutually independent groups. For example, let's compare the means for the **model 1** and **model 2** fridge sales and check whether there is any statistically significant difference between the two:

```
ttest fridge_sales, by(model)
```

In this case, the command will check the distributions and means of both the models with respect to the sales of the fridges data. The result of the query will look like this:

```
Two-sample t test with equal variances
----------------------------------------------------------------------------
Group     | Obs     Mean     Std. Err.   Std.Dev.   [95% Conf. Interval]
model 1   |    40   9502     1.8764      20.345     9499.98   9506.23
model 2   |    60   9820     0.9873      18.987     9815.12   9824.84
----------------------------------------------------------------------------
Combined  |   100   9692.8   9692.8      9692.8     9692.8    9692.8
----------------------------------------------------------------------------
diff      |         -318     0.8891                 -318      -318
----------------------------------------------------------------------------
Degrees of freedom: 98

Ho: mean(model1) - mean(model2) = diff = 0

Ha: diff < 0              Ha: diff ~= 0            Ha: diff > 0
t = -2.345               t = -2.345               t = -2.345
P < t = 0.0001           P > |t| = 0.0004         P > t = 0.8888
```

This shows that there is a significant difference between the means of the two groups in question. Here is how you calculate the two sample t test:

$$t = \frac{\bar{X}_1 - \bar{X}_2}{s_{X_1 X_2} \cdot \sqrt{\frac{1}{n}}}$$

where

$$s_{X_1 X_2} = \sqrt{(s_{X_1}^2 + s_{X_2}^2)}$$

The chi-square goodness of fit test

The chi-square (the goodness of fit check) gives you the option to test whether proportions of observed values statistically differ from the values in the hypothesis population proportions.

The chi-square statistical test is generally leveraged to compare the observed data with the hypothesized data. It also gives you an idea about the goodness of fit before you start with the modeling exercise. It checks for the deviations between different samples of the observed data, what we believe the data would look like, and what insights the data will have. The chi-square test gives you the deviation with respect to a null hypothesis.

For example, let's assume that the inventory of fridges consists of 20% **model1**, 20% **model2**, 10% **model3**, and 50% **model4**. We need to check whether the observed data has proportions in the sample data. For such problems, you need to run a chi-square test of the goodness of fit. Here is how you perform the chi-square test for the goodness of fit:

```
csmgof model, expperc(20 20 10 50)
```

The `csmgof` command is a user defined command and is not readily available in Stata. Here are the results of the command:

Model	expprc	expfreq	obsfreq
model1	20	25	
model2	20	15	
model3	10	15	
model4	50	45	

chisq (3) is 5.03, p = .1765

This output shows that the composition of the fridge inventory does not differ significantly from the values in the preceding hypothesis (the chi-square test with **3 degrees of freedom, that is, 5.03, p = .1765**).

ANOVA

Analysis of variance (ANOVA), also known as the one-way analysis of variance, is generally leveraged if your data includes a categorical variable that is an independent variable (with more than one category). The variable in question should be a normally distributed variable and an interval-dependent variable. ANOVA checks for the various means at the different levels defined by the independent variable. Here is how you can run ANOVA in Stata:

```
anova fridge_sales model
```

Here are the results of this query:

Source		Partial SS	df	MS	F	Prob > F
		Number of obs = 100			R-squared = 0.19876	
		Root MSE = 9.3478			Adj R-squared = 0.1734	
Model	|	9875.897	2	1987.345	19.234	0.0000
Model	|	9875.897	2	1987.345	19.234	0.0001
Residual	|	39503.588	97	89.999		
Total	|	49379.485	99	102.334		

Now, let's work on the model and summarized results of the fridge sales with respect to the model types.

The average or mean of the dependent variable is significantly different from each other. However, now the problem is that we don't have an exact idea about the quantitative difference between the model types. Here is the command to check the differences between the model types:

```
tabulate model, summarize(fridge_sale)
```

Here are the results of this query:

type of model		Summary of fridge sales		
		Mean	Std. Dev.	Freq.
Model1	|	9856.97	10.234	30
Model2	|	9765.23	11.234	50
Model3	|	9512	12.349	20
Total	|	9711.4	11.27233	100

One-way repeated ANOVA measures

We can perform a one-way repeated measure of ANOVA (analysis of variance) if we have the following:

- A variable that is categorically independent
- A variable that is normally distributed and interval-dependent

These variables need to be repeated two times or more for each type.

This is a test similar to the paired sample t test, but this test gives you the option to run ANOVA for two or more types of categories in the variable. It checks whether the mean of the dependent variable is statistically different with respect to the categorical variable.

Here is the command to run such a test:

```
anova   B   A   C,     repeated(A)
```

Here are the results of this query:

	Number of obs = 100			R-squared = 0.7523	
	Root MSE = 1.2346			Adj R-squared = 0.7034	
Source	Partial SS	df	MS	F	Prob > F
Model	83.23	10	7.34	6.345	0.0003
A	40.23	3	17.23	12.46	0.0002
C	29.34	7	3.65	4.01	0.0120
Residual	30.12	21	1.2367		
Total	99.69	31	2.4133		

Between-subjects error term: C
Levels   : 8   (7 df)
Lowest b.s.e variable   : C

Repeated variable: A

		Huynh-Feldt epsilon		= 0.8528
Greenhouse-Geisser epsilon		= 0.6234
Box's conservative epsilon		= 0.3412

```
                        --------------------------Prob > F------------------------
  Source   |    df       F      Regular     H-F        G-G        Box

    A      |     3     10.23    0.0001    0.0002     0.0012     0.0234
  Residual |    21
         --------------------------------------------------------------------------
```

In this case, there are four different p-values, as shown in the preceding figure. Regular is the p-value you generally get if the assumption of compound symmetry is *true* in the case of a given dataset. P-values in the **Huynh-Feldt (H-F)** test, **Greenhouse-Geisser (G-G)** test and Box's conservative test and Box test. The preceding figure shows that we have a statistically significant effect on the p-value of `0.05`.

MANOVA

MANOVA is also known as a **multivariate analysis of variance**. This test is similar to ANOVA, but in the case of MANOVA, you have two or more than two dependent variables.

In one-way MANOVA, there are the following:

- A categorical variable that is independent
- Dependant variables (two or more)

Here is a Stata command for MANOVA:

```
manova sales cost size = model, category(model)
```

Here are the results of this query:

```
Number of obs = 100
   W = Wilks' lambda          L = Lawley-Hotelling trace
   P = Pillai's trace         R = Roy's largest root
```

Source	Statistic		df	F(df1,	df2) =	F	Prob>F	
model	Model 1	0.6823	2	5.0	380.0	11.45	0.0000	e
	Model 2	0.2345		5.0	382.0	11.23	0.0000	a
	Model3	0.3867		5.0	398.0	12.23	0.0000	a
	Model 4	0.3425		3.0	200.0	22.87	0.0000	u
Residual			97					
Total			99					

e = exact, a = approximate, u = upper bound on F

Here is the mathematical derivation for MANOVA:

- Samuel Stanley Wilks' formula is as follows:

$$\Lambda_{Wilks} = \prod_{1...p}(1/(1+\lambda_p)) = \det(I+A)^{-1} = \det(\Sigma_{res})/\det(\Sigma_{res}+\Sigma_{model})$$

- The Pillai-M. S. Bartlett trace formula is as follows:

$$\Lambda_{Pillai} = \sum_{1...p}(\lambda_p/(1+\lambda_p)) = \mathrm{tr}((I+A)^{-1})$$

- The Lawley-Hotelling trace formula is as follows:

$$\Lambda_{LH} = \sum_{1...p}(\lambda_p) = \mathrm{tr}(A)$$

- Roy's greatest root formula is as follows:

$$\Lambda_{Roy} = max_p(\lambda_p) = \|A\|_\infty$$

Fisher's exact test

Fisher's exact test is utilized when there is a need for a chi-square test, but one or more than one row in your observation dataset have five or less values in terms of frequency. The basic assumption in a chi-square test is that the frequency of the values in the rows of the given dataset is five or more than five. Fisher's exact test does not need this assumption:

```
tabulate model fridge_type,
exact
```

Here are the results of this query:

Type of fridge	Model1	Model2	Model3	Model4	Total
Old	20	11	34	123	188
New	3	2	12	43	188
Total	23	23	23	23	

Fisher's exact = 0.652

This outcome tells you that `fridge_type` and model are not statistically related (that is p is equal to *0.652*). Fisher's test computes the p-value directly. Here is the mathematical derivation of the fisher's test:

Look at the following assumed data of fridge sales:

	Old	New	Row Total
Model1	a	b	a + b
Model2	c	d	c + d
Column Total	a + c	b + d	a + b + c + d (=n)

Then, the probability and the **p** value is given by the following formula:

$$p = \frac{\binom{a+b}{a}\binom{c+d}{c}}{\binom{n}{a+c}} = \frac{(a+b)!\ (c+d)!\ (a+c)!\ (b+d)!}{a!\ b!\ c!\ d!\ n!}$$

The Wilcoxon-Mann-Whitney test

The **Wilcoxon-Mann-Whitney** test is known for its **nonparametric analog,** where the t test (the independent samples) can be leveraged if there is no assumption of a dependent variable being a normally distributed variable and where the variable is just an ordinary variable. This is one of the reasons why the Stata code for the Wilcoxon-Mann-Whitney test is similar to that of an independent sample t test. Here is an example:

```
ranksum fridge_sales,
by(model)
```

Here are the results of this query:

```
Two-sample Wilcoxon rank-sum (Mann-Whitney) test

-------------------------------------------------------------------------------
   Model    |        obs              rank sum               expected
-------------------------------------------------------------------------------
   Model1   |        90                 7800                  8523.98
   Model2   |        103                10983                 12567.34
-------------------------------------------------------------------------------
  combined  |        193                 193                   193


              unadjusted variance            198237.45
              adjustment for ties             -987.45
                                         ------------------
              adjusted variance               197250

       Ho: fridge_Sales(model1==model2) = fridge_sales(model1==model1)
                                z = -4.329
```

In this case, here is the mathematical formula:

$$z = \frac{U - m_U}{\sigma_U},$$

Here, **U** is referring to normally distributed variables in the given dataset.

$$m_U = \frac{n_1 n_2}{2}, \text{ and}$$

$$\sigma_U = \sqrt{\frac{n_1 n_2 (n_1 + n_2 + 1)}{12}}.$$

n1 and **n2** are the number of observations in the related datasets.

Summary

Statistical tests, such as t tests, the chi-square test, ANOVA, MANOVA, and Fisher's test, are significant in terms of the exercise of model building. The more the tests you conduct on the given data, the better understanding you get of the data; you can also check how different variables interact with each other.

These variable interactions and the understanding and significance at various levels come really handy when developing different models.

5
Linear Regression in Stata

One of the most used techniques in analytics is linear regression. It helps you predict values based on independent variables. Stata has one of the simplest syntaxes for linear regression and it can prove to be the best tool for predictive analytics and statistical modeling as far as linear regression is concerned. Stata's simple syntax makes it easy for users to understand and relate to statistical (linear regression) concepts and apply these concepts in real life successfully. This will be your first chapter that will foray into statistical modeling, and it's an extremely important chapter from the point of view of developing good knowledge of modeling.

Here are some of the topics we will cover in this chapter:

- Linear regression
- The linear regression code in Stata
- The variance inflation factor and multicollinearity
- Homoscedasticity

Linear regression

Let's first understand what linear regression is. It is an effort to model and find out the existing linear relationship between given variables by fitting a linear equation to the observed data of given variables. One of the variables is considered to be dependent variable, and others are considered to be independent variables or explanatory variables. Linear regression is a technique that's used industry-wide. It is one of the most famous techniques in the analytics industry and has a lot of uses, such as the prediction of any continuous variables—rainfall, sales, sensor outputs, loan default amount, and so on.

Linear regression is one of the simplest techniques as well. It is widely used in healthcare, FMCG/CPG/retain goods, finance, marketing, and so on. There are various linear regression methods that are listed as you read the chapter in detail. One of the most leveraged methods is the ordinary least squares method. This chapter will prepare you for statistical modeling and predictive modeling in Stata through linear regression. You can leverage the knowledge from this chapter directly into your daily work life. Look at the following figure; it shows the curve-fitting line of regression for the given points:

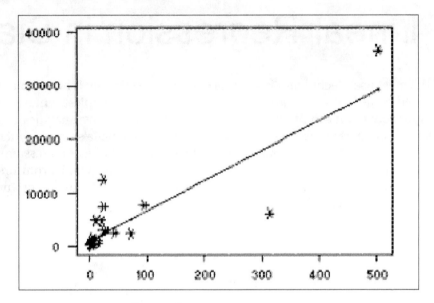

This line of regression tried to capture all the relevant points and tried to be as close to these points as possible. Now, any value of x can predict the value of y. This is the simplest form of linear regression. There are various types of linear regressions, such as the following:

- Ordinary least squares
- Generalized least squares
- Percentage least squares
- Iteratively reweighted least squares
- Instrumental variables
- Optimal instruments
- Total least squares
- Maximum likelihood estimation
- Ridge regression

- Least absolute deviation
- Adaptive estimation
- Bayesian linear regression
- Quantile regression
- Mixed models
- Principal component regression
- Least-angle regression
- The Theil–Sen estimator

In this chapter, we will mostly concentrate on ordinary least squares, and we will show some Stata code to run other type of linear regressions.

Here are some of the assumptions we make while running linear regression:

- **Normal distribution**: Errors are assumed to be normally distributed. Technically speaking, the normality of the data is one of the primary necessities for hypothesis tests to be good enough to be tested.

- **Linear relationship**: The predicting and predicted variables should have a linear relationship. This is one of the most crucial requirements. The errors should be identically distributed for the correct prediction and estimation of coefficients. This distribution needs to be independent as well.

- **Homoscedasticity assumption**: It is assumed that the error variance is constant.

- **Independence assumption**: It is assumed that any of the errors affiliated with the given observation are not correlated at all with the errors of any other given observation.

- **Variable/measurement errors**: Variables that are leveraged to predict the outcomes are measured without any errors.

- **Specification of the model**: The data model needs to be specified properly (this process should include only relevant variables and exclude all nonrelevant variables).

- **Equality of outliers influence assumption**: You need to keep in mind all the individual observations that influence the coefficients drastically.

- **Multicollinearity**: Independent variables that are highly collinear have a bad impact on the model and stability of the coefficients. You need to drop any variables that are collinear and give an additive effect to the model. This is discussed further in the multicollinearity section.

Linear regression code in Stata

Let's venture into the code for linear regression using Stata and assume the following data:

Drug	Sales	Salespeople	GDP	Competitive_Index
Drug1	1029	97	6	5
Drug2	870	80	6.2	4
.	.	.	.	.
.	.	.	.	.
.	.	.	.	.
.	.	.	.	.
.	.	.	.	.
.	.	.	.	.
Drugn	987	50	6.2	5

Here is the data dictionary:

- **Drug**: This is the name of the drug
- **Sales**: This is the number of drugs/medicines sold in a month
- **Salespeople**: This is the number of sales people required to support sales operations and activities for the given drug
- **GDP**: This is the GDP of the given territory
- **Competitive_Index**: This tells us how competitive the market for this drug is

Now, we need to find the relation between sales and figure how it is related to other variables such as salespeople, GDP, and competitive index. Here is the Stata code for this:

```
regress sales salespeople GDP Competitve_index
```

The results of the preceding Stata code are as follows:

```
  Source |      SS         df        MS
---------|--------------------------------------
   Model |  287398.45      5      72639.23
Residual |   18293.43     287      5898.34
---------|--------------------------------------
   Total |  305691.88     292      78537.57
```

This code is case-sensitive. Take a look at the following code:

```
regress sales SAlespeople GDP Competitve_index
```

If you type the preceding code, it will give you the following error:

Variable Salespeople not found

So, you need to be careful while writing the code and make sure the case sensitivity is accounted for in the code. In this case, the total degrees of freedom are *292*, which is *1* less than the total number of observations. In this data, the total number of observations is *293*.

The **R-squared** variable of the model, as shown in the following figure, is *0.7891*, which means that the model explains 79% variability in the dependent or target variable. The **Adj R-squared** is *0.7810* and **Root MSE** is *63.145*.

Number of obs	=	293
F(5,287)	=	213.45
Prob > F	=	0.0000
R-squared	=	0.7891
Adj R-squared	=	0.7810
Root MSE	=	63.145

The following figure is part of the output from Stata. It gives you the coefficient of the variables, their standard errors, t values, and the significance levels. This table is the crux of the regression, and we need to understand it very carefully.

Sales	Coef.	Std. Err.	t	P>|t|	[95% Conf. Interval]	
salespeople	2.7865	1.986359	-1.67	0.003	-4.298537	0.048392
GDP	-1.657	0.47293	-18.34	0.000	-2.386783	0.037486
Competitive_index	-0.3587	0.18279	3.2	0.298	-0.092378	0.384672
_cons	200.357	34.872	15.3492	0.000	764.2345	872.3564

Looking at the preceding output, all the variables seem to be significant, except **Competitive_index**, which is at a significance level of *0.05* (significance level equal to *0.298*). The **Salespeople** variable has a significance level of *0.003* and passes through our criteria. It has a coefficient value of *2.7865*, which is on the positive side. So, the more the number of sales people working on the sales operations and other activities, the better the sales results. In similar way, **GDP** has a coefficient of *-1.657*, which is negative. So, the more the **GDP**, the lesser you spend on healthcare and drug purchase. More **GDP** implies better health and more healthy people.

You can also try using the GUI for linear regression in Stata. The following screenshot will show you how to carry out linear regression in Stata:

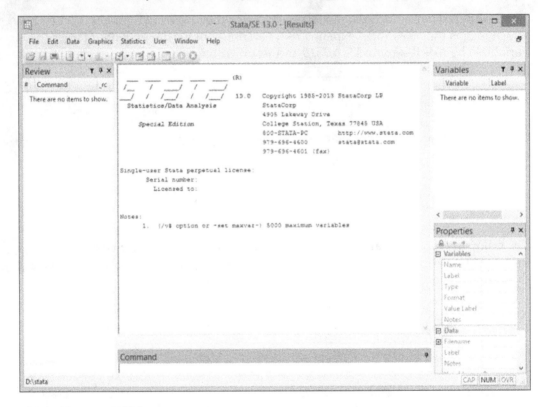

After clicking on the **Statistics** menu, you can see the different options, as follows:

When you click on **Linear regression**, you will be prompted to navigate to **Linear regression | Regress box**, as follows:

You can select **Dependent variables** and **Independent variables** in the given box and perform the linear regression analysis as follows:

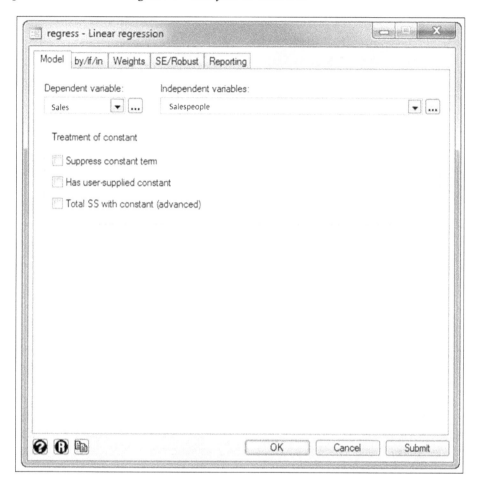

This gives you the same output as the one given by the code shown in the following figure:

Number of obs	= 293
F(5,287)	= 213.45
Prob > F	= 0.0000
R-squared	= 0.7891
Adj R-squared	= 0.7810
Root MSE	= 63.145

Source	SS	df	MS
Model	287398.45	5	72639.23
Residual	18293.43	287	5898.34
Total	305691.88	292	78537.57

Sales	Coef.	Std. Err.	t	P>|t|	[95% Conf. Interval]	
salespeople	2.7865	1.986359	-1.67	0.003	-4.298537	0.048392
GDP	-1.657	0.47293	-18.34	0.000	-2.386783	0.037486
Competitive_index	-0.3587	0.18279	3.2	0.298	-0.092378	0.384672
_cons	200.357	34.872	15.3492	0.000	764.2345	872.3564

Variance inflation factor and multicollinearity

What if your independent variables are related to each other, for example, the date of birth and age? Both variables are related to each other or can be derived with one variable. In this case, the regression equation will have an additive effect due to similarities between the variables; the value of the predicted values can be inflated. This condition is called **multicollinearity**. It can be treated using **variance inflation factor (VIF)** The VIF for the given variable indicates how correlated it is compared to other variables. The preceding VIF cutoffs are considered to be multicollinear, which are set at industry level. Healthcare and marketing data generally have a cutoff of 3. Each variable that has a VIF higher than 3 is considered to be multicollinear and is dropped from the model. In the case of multicollinearity, coefficients of the variables become unstable and standard errors are inflated.

Here is the Stata code to detect multicollinearity and find the VIF values at the variable level:

```
regress sales salespeople gdp competitve_index
vif
```

The `vif` command gives you the following results:

Variable	VIF	1/VIF
salespeople	2.34	0.427350
gdp	2.41	0.414938
competitive_index	1.34	0.746269
Mean VIF	2.03	

In the preceding figure, all the variables have the VIF below 3 (that is, *2.34*, *2.41*, and *1.34*)

This means that multicollinearity is within limits and under control. Hence, we do not have to drop any variable. What if one of the VIFs was greater than 3? In that case, you would have to drop the variable with a VIF above 3 and rerun the model.

Homoscedasticity

One of the major assumptions given for type ordinary least squares regression is the homogeneity in the case of variance of the residuals. In the case of a well-fitted model, if you plot residual values versus fitted values, you should not see any particular pattern. Now, what if the variance given by the residuals is not a constant? In this case, the **residual variance** is called **heteroscedastic**. You can detect the heteroscedasticity in various graphical and non-graphical ways.

The most commonly used way to detect heteroscedasticity is by plotting residuals versus predicted values. In Stata, we can perform this using the rvfplot command. When we leverage the rvfplot command with the option of yline(0), which is defining the basis of Y equal to 0, we can see that the data point pattern can get narrower as we move toward the right-hand side. This indicates that heteroscedasticity exists:

```
rvfplot, yline(0)
```

After running the preceding code, you get the following diagram:

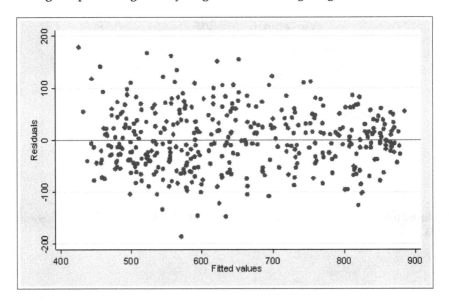

One of the best techniques to identify heteroscedasticity is the **IM test**. It gives you the Cameron and Trivedi' decomposition using the IM test. It also gives you the following measures:

- Heteroscedasticity
- Skewness
- Kurtosis

The IM test word in the code suggests that Stata run the Cameron and Trivedi test on the given data. This test is extremely helpful in identifying heteroscedasticity. You can also write the following code to control heteroscedasticity:

```
regress sales salespeople GDP Competitve_index, robust
```

The word `robust` is written to control the heteroscedasticity of the data. Here is an example of the Stata code for heteroscedasticity:

```
estat imtest
```

When you run the preceding code in Stata, you get the following results:

Cameron & Trivedi's decomposition of IM-test			
Source	chi2	df	p
Heteroskedasticity	16.25	8	0.0237
Skewness	6.34	4	0.0214
Kurtosis	0.23	1	0.5721
Total	22.82	13	0.2057

Another command in Stata can be `hettest`:

```
estat hettest
```

`hettest` gives you the chi-square values and the significance value of the null hypothesis. The output is shown as follows:

```
Breusch-Pagan / Cook-Weisberg test for heteroskedasticity
    Ho:              Constant variance
    Variables:       fitted values of sales
    chi2(1)      =   7.47
    Prob > chi2  =   0.0028
```

IM test is the first test to check the heteroscedasticity. The second test is HET test, which is also known as **Breusch-Pagan test**.

In both the tests, we have the null hypothesis that homogeneousness of the the variance of the residuals exists. In this case, the p-value is going to be very small (almost negligible). In such cases, the best way is to reject the hypothesis and accept the second hypothesis that the variance is nonhomogenous.

These tests are extremely sensitive to the assumptions made while building the model, such as the normality of the data. In the preceding case, heteroscedasticity does not exist.

Checking the heteroscedasticity of the model is a really important step in linear regression. In order to successfully build an optimized model, you have to run the tests and reject the null hypothesis as required.

Summary

In this chapter, you learned about linear regression methods and their assumptions. You also got to know about all the nitty-gritty, such as multicollinearity, heteroscedasticity, and so on. In next chapter, we will discuss logistic regression in detail. An overview of this chapter will help you understand logistic regression in a better way.

6
Logistic Regression in Stata

In this chapter, we will learn about logistic/binary regression. Logistic regression is a really important concept when it comes to knowing about the probability of a particular event happening, for example, whether a particular customer will default on their loan payments, whether it will rain on given day, whether a telecom customer will pay the bill on time, and so on. In order to understand logistic regression better, let's discuss linear regression with **Online Linguistic Support (OLS)**. OLS is leveraged to determine or predict the quantity of data or the quantified value of variables. However, logistic regression is leveraged to determine whether the data values will give the result in a code format from 0 to 1. In simpler words, based on the data, logistic regression predicts whether an event will happen or not.

In this chapter, we will cover the following aspects of logistic regression:

*   The logistic regression concept
*   Logistic regression in Stata
*   Logistic regression for finance (loans and credit cards)

The logistic regression concept

Let's discuss some random data of rainfall from 2000 to 2011. In 2010, there was rainfall, and we have to find out about the probability of rainfall in 2011. So, logistic regression will predict whether the rainfall will happen or not, and OLS will predict the amount of rainfall in that year.

The data we'll look at in this example will tell us more about the dissimilarity between OLS and logistic regression. We will take the rainfall data for 2011 in this case.

To understand the exact difference between linear and logistic regression, let's see what happens if the data that has a binary outcome variable (*event will happen = 1* and *event will not happen = 0*) is analyzed by leveraging linear regression. Let's take the dataset where you need to predict whether the fridge model will be sold above the cutoff or not. In this case, the dependent variable is called `fridge_sales`. This variable is created from the `fridge_actual_sales` variable, which is a continuous variable. Let's say the fridge sales have a cutoff of *1000*. If the fridge sales are above *1000* fridges, then the campaign is successful; otherwise, it's not. So, the values *above 1000* are coded as *1* and the values *below 1000* are coded as *0*. Now, you can run linear regression or OLS on this data and check the results. This is the homework for you to understand the importance of logistic regression.

Logit

In this section, we will review some of the languages involved in logit; this is also called **jargon**. Some of the terms involved are probability, odds, odds ratio, and log odds:

- **Probability**: This defines how an event will happen. Let's consider an example of a coin; after tossing the coin, you will get either heads or tales. So, its probability will be ½.

- **Odds**: This defines the chance that an event will happen or not. For this, we have to divide *chances will happen* by *chances will not happen*. For example, we will take an earlier example top. As we have seen, ½ is the probability of *top will rotate* and let's assume ½ is the probability of *top will not rotate*. Hence, *1/2/1/2=1*.

- **The odds ratio**: This is a ratio of two odds. To understand this term, we will take an example of two schools that wish to unite for a game. One school has *35% boys* who want to play cricket, and the other one has *45% girls* who want to play cricket.

- **Log odds**: This is a logarithm of odds; figures of logistics regression are expressed in log odds. As the figures are expressed in log odds, in this one, the figure will change (the predictor variable) whereas all other variable will remain constant.

- **The formcalc command**: Also known as the **odds ratio command**, this is used to find the odds ratio. In Stata, this can be done by going to the help page and typing `findit Orcalc`. Also, it's very handy to use; just insert the probabilities of set 3 and set 4. This is a user defined command and not the official Stata command. Here is an example:

```
Ormcalc .5 .6
Odds ratio for set 4 and set 3
Odds ratio = P4/ (1-P4)
                    P3/ (1-P3)
```

Now, let's try to insert values for *P4* and *P3* in the preceding formula; this can be seen as follows:

```
Odds ratio =        0.50 (1-0.50)        0.50 0.625
                    0.20 (1-0.20)        0.80
```

As we know. logistic regression is binary and data variables are denoted as *0* and *1*. Also, the code should be in numbers; it is necessary that *0* be given to the *event that will not happen* and *1* to the *event that may happen*. Logistic regression can only be done on data variables (*0, 1*). It is very important to note that Stata will consider all dependent variable values as *0* and *1*; therefore the data containing values other than 0 and 1, needs to be converted into 0 and 1 before performing logistic regression.

Here are the requirements of logistic regression:

- An outcome variable with two possible categorical outcomes (*1=success; 0=failure*)
- A way to estimate the probability *P* of the outcome variable
- A way to link the outcome variable to the explanatory variables
- A way to test the goodness of fit of the regression model

The outcome you get from logistic regression, which is a number between *0* and *1*, is an odds ratio that is given in the left-hand side of the following equation:

$$\text{logit}(p_i) = \log\left(\frac{p_i}{1-p_i}\right)$$

where

i is the indexes of all cases (observations).

p_i is the probability the event (a sale, for example) occurs in the ith case.

log   is the natural log (to the base e).

The *logit (Pi)* can also be written as follows:

$$\log \frac{p(x)}{1 - p(x)} = \beta_0 + x \cdot \beta$$

The preceding equation can be rearranged in the following form:

$$p(x; b, w) = \frac{e^{\beta_0 + x \cdot \beta}}{1 + e^{\beta_0 + x \cdot \beta}} = \frac{1}{1 + e^{-(\beta_0 + x \cdot \beta)}}$$

This can be graphically represented as follows:

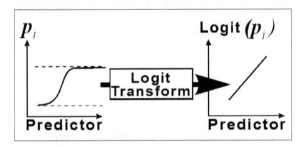

The ways in which you can interpret the coefficients and parameters in a given logistic regression are as follows:

- The sign (±) of β specifies whether the log of odds of y has an increasing or decreasing pattern (for a 1-unit increment or decrement in x)
- If β is greater than 0, then there is an assumed and observed increment in the calculated log of the odds of y for every given 1-unit increment in x
- If β is less than 0, then there is an assumed or observed decrement in the calculated log odds of y for every given 1-unit increment in x
- If β is equal to 0, then no linear relationship is seen between the calculated log of odds and the given values of x

For example, the most simplified model in healthcare is shown as follows. It is a simple model that leverages only three risk factors (weight, sex, and the blood sugar level). This model is built to predict the 10-year health risk of death because of heart failure. Here are the parameters and coefficients:

```
⊠0 equals to 5.0 (the constant or the intercept)
⊠2 equals to 1.0
⊠3 equal to + 1.2
⊠1 equal to + 2.0
x1 = weight in kilos, above 60
x2 = sex, where 0 is female and 1 is male
x3 = blood sugar level, in mg/dL above 1.0
```

The formula to predict the 10-years health risk of death is as follows:

$$risk\ of\ death = \frac{1}{1 + e^{-z}}, \text{where } z = -5 + 2x_1 - 1x_2 + 1.2\ x_3$$

From the preceding formula, we can understand the following facts:

- Increasing weight is affiliated with an increased risk of heart failure and death (*z* goes up by *2.0* units for every given patient over the weight of *60 kg*)

- The male sex is affiliated with a decrement in the risk of heart failure and death (*z* goes down by *1.0* if the patient sex is male)

- Increasing blood sugar is affiliated with an increment in the risk of heart failure (*z* goes up by *1.2* units for every 1 mg/dL increment in blood sugar above 5 mg/dL)

Let's assume the following numbers about a patient who weighs *50* kg and whose blood sugar level is 7.0 mg/dL. The patient's risk of heart failure is, therefore, as follows:

$$\frac{1}{1 + e^{-z}}, \text{where } z = -5 + 2 * (50 - 50) + (-1) * 0 + (1.2) * (7 - 5)$$

Logistic regression in Stata

The two commands of Stata are the `logit` command and the `logistic` command. The `logit` command demonstrates the coefficient whereas `logistic` demonstrates the odds ratios. One can also find out the odds ratios from the `logit` command through the `or` option. In the second section, we will discuss how coefficients and odds are interrelated and how they can be converted. Now, let's take a look at the logarithm pattern. The logs used in this section are natural logs. An example is *if log (d) = e, then log (8) = 0.90308 exp (0.90308) = 8*; here, `exp` represents exponentiation, and it is essential because it shows the link between the coefficient and odds ratios. To better understand the difference between the `logit` coefficient and the `logit` command, we have built few sets of data; the `tabulate` command is used for their distribution. In OLS regression, predicted values are used and graph a is plotted; we will use the same thing here. An example is given later on in the chapter.

```
clear output a b count.
```

a	b	Count
2	1	11
3	0	1
6	7	0
8	9	4

```
expand count (from above data 40 observations are formed)
```

The `expand` command makes it easy to enter data. In the data we have created, variables a and b represent the values and count represents the repeated values. It depends on an individual how many times they want to repeat the data. As we know, expand makes it easy to enter the data, and the `list` command is used to view it. It is important to note that when the `list` command is used individually, it means that there are no variables; then, Stata will list all the variables by default. Here is an example of the data created, and it is represented through the `list` command:

	a	b	count
1	2	1	30
2	4	2	30
3	5	2	30
4	9	2	30
5	0	2	30
6	0	2	30
7	3	2	30

	a	b	count
8	4	3	30
9	6	4	30
10	8	0	30
11	2	0	30
12	1	0	30
13	0	0	30
14	2	0	30
15	4	0	30
16	6	56	30
17	54	58	30
18	40	87	30
19	20	23	30
20	2	43	30
21	11	22	30
22	12	20	30
23	15	40	30
24	63	80	30
25	22	29	30
26	34	46	30
27	35	74	30
28	68	89	30
29	76	39	30
30	18	87	30
31	56	33	30
32	50	44	30
33	40	55	30
34	30	66	30
35	20	22	30

In the following table, we will use the `tabulate` command:

`tabulate a b , col`

a	b 2	3	Total
2	20	20	40
	30	30	60
3	40	40	80
	60	60	120
Total	70	70	140
	90	90	180

Let's move on to the `logit` command:

`logit b a`

```
Iteration 0: log likelihood = -42. 78890
Iteration 1: log likelihood = -39.89801
Iteration 2: log likelihood = -37.909822
Iteration 3: log likelihood = -37.909844
Logit estimate:
Number of observations = 80
LR ch_chii (3) = 8.99
Prob>ch_chii(3) = 0.1022
Pseudo_dr R4 = 1.073
Loglikelihood = -37.909844
```

b	Coefficient	Stand_ error	z	P> l z l	{95% Con_conf. Interval}
a	1	0.35999	3.79	0.1012	0.243673 7654
Co_ cons	1	0.667809	-1	2	-0.76543 76543

Now, let's look at the logistic command:

logistic b a

    Logistic estimates:
    Number of observations = 80
    LR ch_chii (3) = 8.99
    Prob>ch_chii(3) = 0.1022
    Pseudo_dr R4 = 1.073
    Log likelihood = 37.909844

	Odds ratio	Stand_ error	z	P> l z l	{ 95% con_conf. Interval}
a	2	0.245768	3.79	0.1012	0.32456 1.20345

Logit b, a , or

    Log likelihood = 37.909844
    Logistic estimates:
    Number of observations = 70
    LR ch_chii (3) = 1
    Prob>ch_chii(3) = 1.4
    Pseudo_dr R4 = 0.45

b	Odds ratio	Stand_ error	z	P> l z l	{ 95% con_conf. Interval}
a	2	0.245768	3.79	0.1012	1.23436 1.76543

logit b, a

    Log likelihood = 37.909844
    Logistic estimates:
    Number of observations = 70
    LR ch_chii (3) = 1
    Prob>ch_chii(3) = 1.45
    Pseudo_dr R4 = .45

b	Odds ratio	Stand_ error	z	P> l z l	{95% con_conf. Interval}
a	2	0.245768	3.79	0.1012	1.23436 1.76543

You can also run logistic regression in Stata using the GUI provided, as follows:

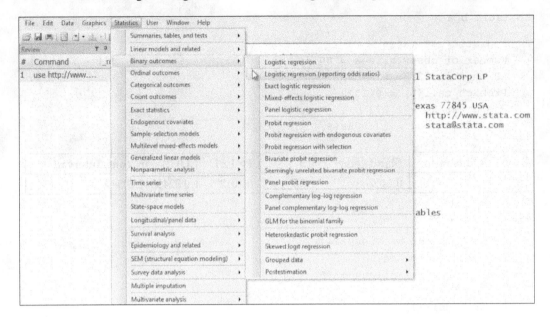

There are a lot of options in **Binary outcomes**. You can select the **Logistic regression tab (reporting odds ratios)** or the **Logistic regression** tab. There are various types of logistic regressions, such as the following:

- **Exact logistic regression**
- **Mixed-effects logistic regression**
- **Panel logistic regression**
- **Probit regression**
- **Bivariate regression** with selection

- **unrelated bivariate probit regression**
- **Panel probit regression**
- **Log-log regression**
- **GLM for the binomial family**

For now, select the simple **Logistic regression** tab. The following tab will open up:

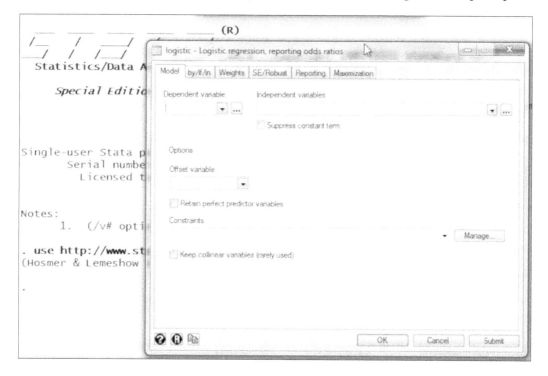

Input the **Dependent** and **Independent** variables in the window, as shown in the following screenshot:

You can also select which type of variable your independent variable is, as shown in the following screenshot:

Your independent variable can be:

- **Factor variable**
- **Time series variable**
- **Simple variable**

Depending on the data and the business objective, you can select the appropriate variable type as your independent variable type:

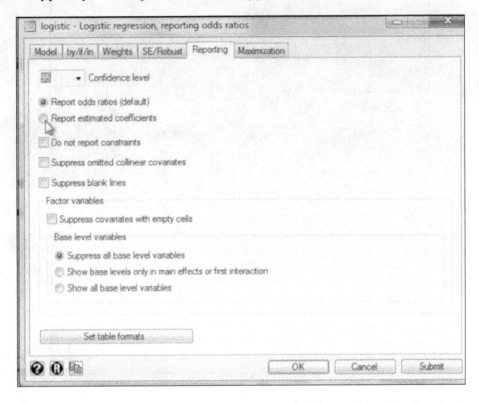

You can select **Report estimate coefficients** as the method to go ahead, which is explained in the next section:

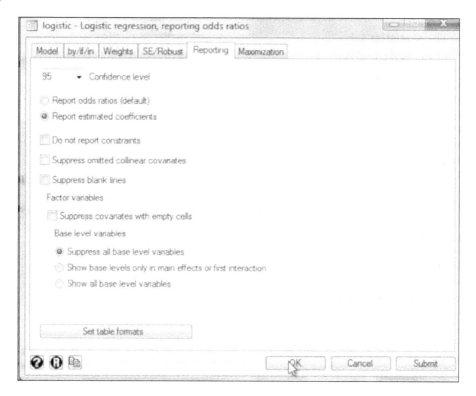

You can also select the **Reporting** tab and select the **Report estimated coefficients** option. This option will give you the details and statistics of estimated coefficients. You can also select the following:

- The **statistics** tab
- In the **statistics** tab, you can select marginal means and predictive means as shown in the following screenshot:

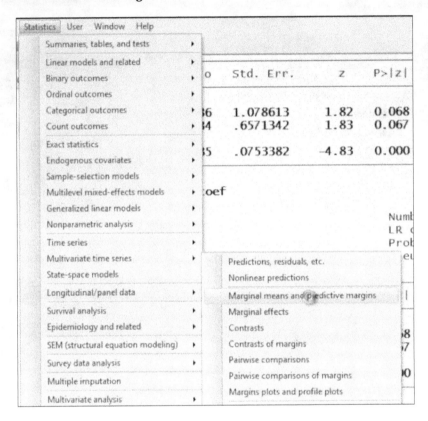

In **margins**, you can add more details about the variable for which you need more details, such as coefficient stability, among other things, as follows:

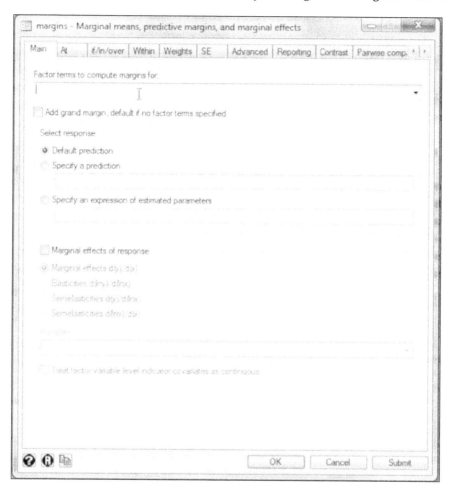

Logistic regression for finance (loans and credit cards)

Logistic regression is heavily used and leveraged in financial domains in order to understand and predict whether a particular customer will pay the loan amount on time and also pay their credit card bills on time. This process is called **application score cards**. In this process, all the demographic details are captured for the customer who has applied for a loan or credit card. Then, the logistic regression model is built on the available past data of existing customers. This model in turn tells us whether the customer who has applied for the loan or credit card will pay their credit card bill or loan installment on time. Majority of the banks leverage the logistic regression structure to answer such business questions.

Summary

In this chapter, you learned how to build a logistic regression model and what the best business situations in which such a model is applied are. It also taught you the theory and application aspects of logistic regression. Finance is the main domain where logistic regression is used to build different kind of score cards.

In last 10 years, the use of logistic regression to predict the risk of a risk for given patient has increased. Apart from healthcare, logistic regression is also used in marketing analytics to predict whether the customer will buy a particular product or not. *Chapter 5, Linear Regression in Stata,* and this chapter cover linear regression and logistic regression, which form the basis of the current analytics industry where two of these modeling techniques are widely used and leveraged in order to make decisions.

Survey Analysis in Stata

Surveys form an important part when it comes to understanding consumer behavior. Analyzing surveys can be tough work given that there are so many questions and you need to get consumer feedback on so many different aspects. In this chapter, we will cover the following aspects of survey analysis:

- Survey analysis concepts
- Survey analysis in Stata (code)
- Sampling

Survey analysis concepts

Many companies and people are hesitant or do not have the bandwidth to conduct surveys. They depend on some of the market research or survey agencies to conduct these surveys, and the results are also analyzed by these agencies. Many of the given estimates and documented standard errors that come from the survey analysis are calculated differently based on various sampling designs and the techniques available in the market. In case of a wrongly specified sampling design, the estimates and the standard errors can go for a toss. This is really crucial in order to understand survey analysis and design.

The following are some of the terminologies and concepts that you need to be well aware of:

- **Weights**: There are various weights assigned during survey design and analysis process. The most common weights among all of these is the sampling weight. Some of the statisticians denote this by **pweight**. It denotes inverse probability on the chances of it being included in the given sample during the process of the sampling design. It is given by the N/n equation, where the following are applicable:

N: The number of observations in the population

n : The number of observations in the sample

So, suppose the population is 20 observations and the random sample is of five observations; then, the pweight or sampling weight is *20/5 = 4*. So, the probability is ¼. This is because there is inverse probability in the first case.

- **Primary sampling unit**: This is the first given unit that is supposed to be sampled as far as the design is concerned. For example, election results in the U.S. need to be sampled. First, we start with Arizona and get a sample of Arizona voters. Then, we replicate this sample design to all the states in the U.S. In this case, the state is the **primary sampling unit**, which is also called **PSU**. The granularity of the samples is decided by the PSUs. Sometimes, you can leverage a probability proportional that fits the sample size design. Cluster sampling is also used in many cases at different levels. However, in case of a given random sample, the units across primary sampling units remain the same.

The following diagram shows you the sampling unit process for a given clinical trial, which is named **NLSY**:

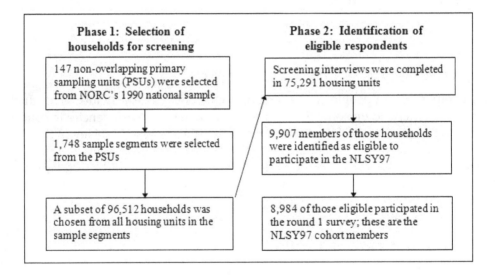

- **Stratification**: This is the best way to divide the population of the given data into different groups or clusters. This can be achieved by leveraging various demographic variables, for example:

```
Gender
Race
Marital status
City
Zip code
State
Country
Age
```

An example of stratification is shown as follows:

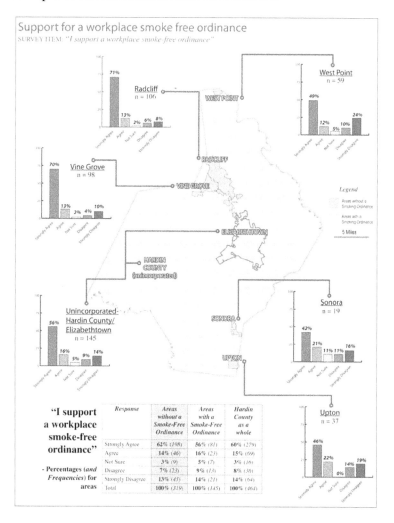

Once you have identified and defined such groups or clusters, you can assume that one sample each from these groups is independent of all other samples of all other groups. For example, let's assume that one sample is withdrawn based on stratification on the basis of gender; this can be either male, female, or other:

In the terms of the pweights language, the pweights for men is going to be different from the pweights for women. Also, a sample taken from the male population is going to be independent of the sample taken from the female population.

So, the purpose of doing this stratification is to make sure that there is an improvement in the accuracy of the estimates provided. When the variable of the selected dependent variable is much smaller for a given strata as compared to the whole population or sample, the effect of stratification is much higher and gives you much more accuracy. An example of a stratified sample is shown in the following figure:

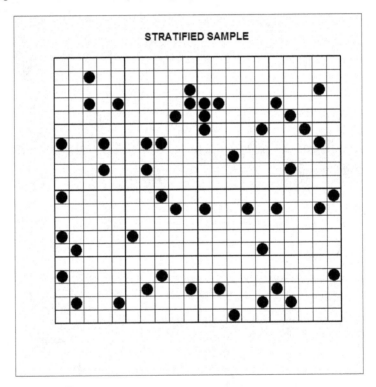

- **FPC**: This means finite population correction. Whenever the sampling fraction is very large, you should use FPC.

 Sampling faction is defined as the number of respondents that are sampled as compared to the population.

FPC is highly leveraged in the standard error calculation for a given estimate. The formula for the FPC calculation is as follows:

$$\text{Fraction} = (N-n)/(N-1)$$
$$\text{FPC} = \text{fraction } \frac{1}{2}$$

So, effectively, FPC is as follows:

$$\text{FPC} = \left((N-n)/(N-1)\right)1/2$$

Here, the following are applicable:

N : Population observations or elements

n : Sample observations or elements

An example is shown as follows:

	A	B
1	Sample Size for Estimating the Mean	
2		
3	Population Standard Deviation	25
4	Sampling Error	5
5	Confidence Level	95%
6	Z Value	-1.95996108
7	Calculated Sample Size	96.03618611
8	Sample Size Needed	97
9		
10		
11	Finite Populations	
12	Population Size	5000
13	Sample Size with FPC	94.24485185
14	Sample Size Needed	95

Survey analysis in Stata code

Let's understand the Stata code to take a random sample from the survey data.
A random sample is also called **simple random sample (SRS)**:

```
use survey_data, clear
count
1095
set seed 2087620
sample 26
count
286
```

The following diagram represents the random sample generation mechanism:

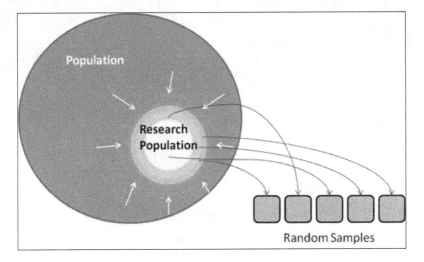

Let's understand how to create pweights that are probability weights for the given sample.

Now, the sampling fraction in our case is given by the following:

$$n / N = 286 / 1095$$
$$\sim 26$$

So, the Stata code for `pweight` is as follows:

```
gen pweight = 1095/286
```

Similarly, FPC will be generated as follows:

```
gen fpc = 1095
```

This command generates the following output:

```
svyset [pweight=pweight], fpc(fpc)

      pweight: pweight
          VCE: linearized
    Strata 1: <one>
        SU 1: <observations>
       FPC 1: fpc
```

Now, we can leverage svyset, which is a command to give out the information stored in Stata with respect to the sampling design and plan. In this case, the PSU numbers remain the same, which means that Stata has a thorough understanding, which is similar to the understanding we have. As there is only one Stata, the sampling design is similar — in fact, it's the same as the one we designed. The svyset command makes sure that Stata stores and remembers the sampling plan and design information throughout the session and is not limited to the code snippet that we have written. When you save the data file, Stata saves the entire survey log or survey information along with it, which is really helpful in order to perform various survey operations in Stata.

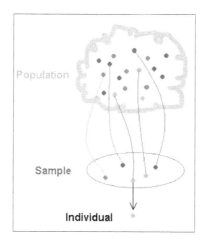

Let's take an example, as shown in the following screenshot:

```
svydes

Survey: Describing stage 1 sampling units


          pweight: pweight
              VCE: linearized
         Strata 1: <one>
           SU 1: <observations>
          FPC 1: fpc
```

The output of this command will be as follows:

```
#Obs per Unit
-----------------------------------------------------
Stratum   #Units    #Obs      min     mean     max
-------   --------  --------  -------  ------   ----
1         286       286       1        1.0      1
-------   --------  --------  -------  ----------
1         286       286       1        1.0      1
-----------------------------------------------------
```

Let's initiate the analysis of the given data files by extracting some basic and descriptive types of statistics. We can leverage the following:

- `svy: mean`
- `svy: total`

The commands available in Stata are as follows:

- The `svy: mean` command: This is generally leveraged to estimate the mean value of the variable in the given population. In our example, we will estimate the mean for `fridge_sales` and volume:

$$svy : mean\ fridge\_sales\ volume$$
$$(running\ mean\ on\ estimation\ sample)$$
$$Survey : Mean\ estimation$$
$$Number\ of\ strata = 1 \quad Number\ of\ obs = 286$$
$$Number\ of\ PSUs = 286 \quad Population\ size = 1095$$
$$Design\ df = 285$$

The output of this will be as follows

```
----------------------------------------------------------
             |              Linearized
             |   Mean   Std. Err.   [95% Conf.Interval]
-------------+--------------------------------------------
Fridge_sales |287.8752  6.298762   280.9836   300.7639
      volume |23.9826   1.865347   20.76398   30.87392
----------------------------------------------------------
```

- The `svy: total` command: This command is leveraged to get all the estimates of all the totals at population levels:

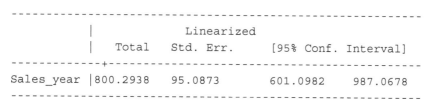

$$\text{svy : total yr rnd}$$
$$(\text{running total on estimation sample})$$
$$\text{Survey : Total estimation}$$
$$\text{Number of strata} = 1 \quad \text{Number of obs} = 286$$
$$\text{Number of PSUs} = 286 \quad \text{Population size} = 1095$$
$$\text{Design df} = 285$$

The output of this command will be as follows:

```
----------------------------------------------------------
             |              Linearized
             |   Total   Std. Err.     [95% Conf. Interval]
-------------+--------------------------------------------
Sales_year  |800.2938  95.0873       601.0982   987.0678
----------------------------------------------------------
```

Let's perform multiple regression on this data file. We can use `fridge_sales` as the dependent variable, volume, and length as independent variables in the model:

$$\text{svy : reg fridge\_sales volume length}$$
$$(\text{running regress on estimation sample})$$
$$\text{Survey : Linear estimation}$$
$$\text{Number of strata} = 1 \quad \text{Number of obs} = 286$$
$$\text{Number of PSUs} = 286 \quad \text{Population size} = 1095$$
$$\text{Design df} = 285$$
$$F(2, 284) = 498.02$$
$$\text{Prob} > F = 0.0000$$
$$\text{R-squared} = 0.7534$$

The output of this command will be as follows:

```
------------------------------------------------------------------
            |              Linearized
fridge_Sales|Coef.      Std. Err.    t      P>|t|  [95% Conf. Interval]
------------+-----------------------------------------------------
volume      |50.98652    8.987832   4.87    0.000  37.98367   71.17326
length      |-2.982567  .9367821  -23.67    0.000  -2.078367  -3.098367
_cons       |609.9826   21.78256   29.87    0.000  600.9821   625.9836
------------------------------------------------------------------
```

The following figure shows the relationship between independent and dependent variables in single variable regression and multiple regression:

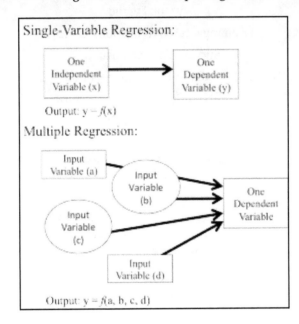

In the broader scope of analytics projects that you may encounter at work, you'll find a lot of datasets apart from survey-related ones. The following diagram is an example of such projects:

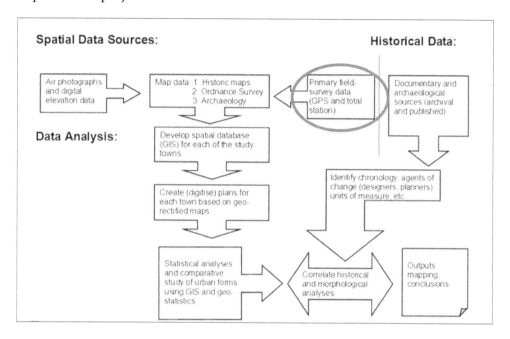

Stratified random sampling is done as follows:

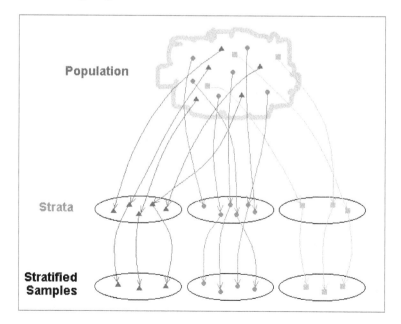

The code to perform random sampling is as follows:

$$svyset, clear(all)$$

$$svyset[pweight = pweight], strata(strataa) fpc(fpc)$$

pweight : pweight

VCE : linearized

Strata 1 : strata

SU 1 :< observations >

FPC 1 : fpc

svydes

Survey : Describing stage 1 sampling units

pweight : pweight

VCE : linearized

Strata 1 : strataa

SU 1 :< observations >

FPC 1 : fpc

The output of this command will be as follows:

```
#Obs per Unit
---------------------------------------------------------------
Stratum    #Units     #Obs       min       mean      max
--------   --------   --------   --------   --------   ---

1          286        286        1         1.0        1
2          286        286        1         1.0        1

--------   --------   --------   -------    --------   ----

2          572        572        1         1.0        1
---------------------------------------------------------------
```

Cluster sampling

Cluster sampling is done as follows:

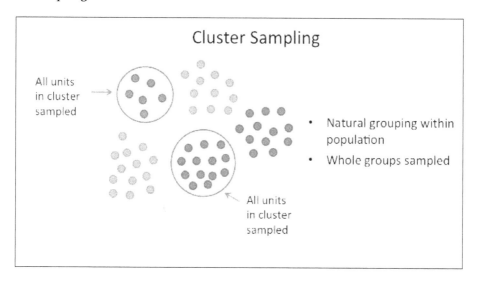

Here is the Stata code to perform cluster sampling:

use surveydata1, clear

svyset data1[pweight = pweight], fpc(fpc)

pweight : pweight

VCE : linearized

Strata1 :< one >

SU1 : data1

FPC1 : fpc

svydes

Survey : Describing stage 1 sampling units

pweight : pweight

VCE : linearized

Strata1 :< one >

SU1 : data1

FPC1 : fpc

The output of this command will be as follows:

```
#Obs per Unit
-----------------------------------------------------------
Stratum    #Units    #Obs    min    mean    max
--------   -------   ------  -----  ------  --------
1           286       286     1      6.1     100
--------   -------   ------  -----  ------  --------
1           286       286     1      6.1     100
-----------------------------------------------------------
```

Here is the code for the mean of the estimation sample:

$$svy : mean \, fridge\_sales \, volume$$
$$(running \, mean \, on \, estimation \, sample)$$
$$Survey : Mean \, estimation$$
$$Number \, of \, strata = 1 \quad Number \, of \, obs = 286$$
$$Number \, of \, PSUs = 20 \quad Population \, size = 1095.28$$
$$Design \, df = 285$$

The output of this code will be as follows:

```
-------------------------------------------------------------------
              |            Linearized
              |   Mean     Std. Err.      [95% Conf. Interval]
--------------+----------------------------------------------------
Fridge_sales  |560.5404    18.08756       540.1245     590.0987
volume        |31.98367    2.983672       25.98367     40.00098
-------------------------------------------------------------------
```

Here is the code to calculate the total of the estimation sample:

$$svy : total \, yr\_sales$$
$$(running \, total \, on \, estimation \, sample)$$
$$Survey : Total \, estimation$$
$$Number \, of \, strata = 1 \quad Number \, of \, obs = 286$$
$$Number \, of \, PSUs = 20 \quad Population \, size = 2095.09$$
$$Design \, df = 285$$

The output of this code will be as follows:

```
-------------------------------------------------------------------
                  |             Linearized
                  |    Total    Std. Err.      [95% Conf. Interval]
------------------+------------------------------------------------
yr_rnd            |  700.0009   100.0099       600.0012     789.009
-------------------------------------------------------------------
```

Summary

In this chapter, we learned about different sampling concepts and methods. We also learned how to implement these methods in Stata. We saw how to apply statistical modeling concepts, such as regression, to the survey data. The next chapter is about time series analysis.

8
Time Series Analysis in Stata

Time series analysis forms an important part of understanding time-based patterns, seasonality and consumer behavior, patient health behavior, and so on. Analyzing time series data can be tough work given there are so many variables and time can be sliced in so many different ways to understand the data and draw insights from the data. We will cover the following aspects of time series analysis in this chapter:

- Time series analysis concepts
- Time series analysis in Stata (code)

Time series analysis concepts

One of the best time series analysis methods is called **ARIMA** or **Box Jenkins**. **ARIMA** stands for **Autoregressive Integrated Moving Averages**.

Unlike regression models, in which Yi is explained by the k regressors ($X1$, $X2$, $X3$, ... , Xk), the BJ-type time series models allow Yi to be explained by past, or lagged, values of Y itself and stochastic error terms.

Let's take a small example of the GDP series, as shown in the following diagram:

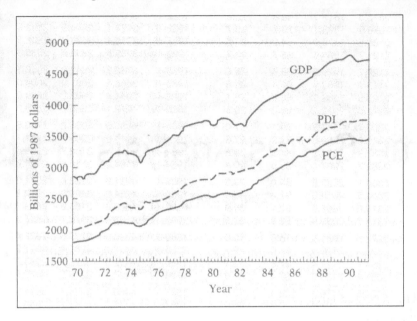

Let's work with the GDP time series data for the United States given in the diagram. A plot of this time series is given in the undifferenced GDP and first-differenced GDP.

In the level form, GDP is nonstationary, but in the first-differenced form, it is stationary. If a time series is stationary, then it can fit the ARIMA model in a variety of ways. A time series is stationary when mean and variance is constant over time. Let's first understand an **autoregressive (AR)** process:

- Let Zt denote the GDP at a given time t.

  This means that we can model Zt as follows:

  $$\left(Zt - \delta\right) = \alpha 1 \left(Zt - 1 - \delta\right) + ut$$

  The preceding formula is defined as follows:

  ○ δ is the mean or the average of Z.

  ○ ut is supposed to be the uncorrelated error term that is completely random and has zero mean. Also, it has constant variance, that is, $o2$ (it is also called white noise).

  ○ Zt follows a first-order autoregressive, or AR(l), stochastic process.

- In this case, the value of Z at a given time t is completely dependent on the value of t in the given time period and is also a random term. So, the Z values are given as deviations from the calculated mean value.

- In simple words, the preceding model states that the forecasted value of Z at the time t is a calculated proportion in a way ($=al$) as compared to its value at the previous time ($t-1$). You need to add a random error or the disturbance at given time t.

- Now, in the given model:

$$(Zt - \delta) = \alpha1(Zt - 1 - \delta) + \alpha2(Zt - 2 - \delta) + ut$$

Zt has a second-order autoregressive order, or the AR(2) process, as shown in the preceding equation.

- The given value of Z at the given time t is dependent on the value of Z in the last two time periods. The values of Z are given around the mean value of δ.

- In general, we have the following formula:

$$(Zt - \delta) = \alpha1(Zt - 1 - \delta) + \alpha2(Zt - 2 - \delta) + \ldots\ldots + \alpha p(Zt - p - \delta) + ut$$

In this case, Zt is a *pth* order autoregressive or AR(*p*) process.

Now, let's understand the **moving averages** process (**MA**):

- Assume that we model Z as follows:

$$Zt = \mu + \beta0ut + \beta1ut - 1$$

The preceding formula is defined as follows:

  - μ is an assumed constant
  - ut is the white noise or a stochastic error term
  - In this case, Z at the given time t is definitely equal to the constant in addition to the moving averages of the current t and past errors: *t-1, t-2*, and so on

Now, in the current scenario, Z is following the moving average that is of the first order, which is also called the MA(1) process.

- Suppose that Z follows this equation:

$$Zt = \mu + \beta 0ut + \beta 1ut - 1 + \beta 2ut - 2$$

This is called an MA(2) process.

On a general note, $Zt = \mu + \beta 0ut + \beta 1ut\text{-}1 + \beta 2ut\text{-}2 + \ldots\ldots + \beta qut\text{-}q$ is an MA(q) process.

We combine both processes in ARIMA:

- AR
- MA

The following figure gives you an overview of the entire ARMA process, which can be converted into ARIMA when you follow the integrated approach:

It is quite possible that Z has certain characteristics of both **AR** and **MA** and is also called **ARMA**.

In this case, Zt is following an ARMA (1, 1) 1,1, process, which can be represented as follows:

$$Zt = \theta + \alpha 1\ Zt - 1 + \beta 0ut + \beta 1ut - 1$$

On a general note, for given orders and the p and q (p, q) process in ARMA, p is the autoregressive term and q is the moving average term. The ARIMA method is explained in the following figure:

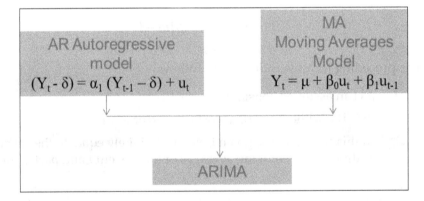

For example, you need to identify key factors affecting the hospital's revenue and forecast the hospital's revenue, that is, the **Gross Collection Rate (GCR)** for the next year. Here is how you execute an ARIMA project at work:

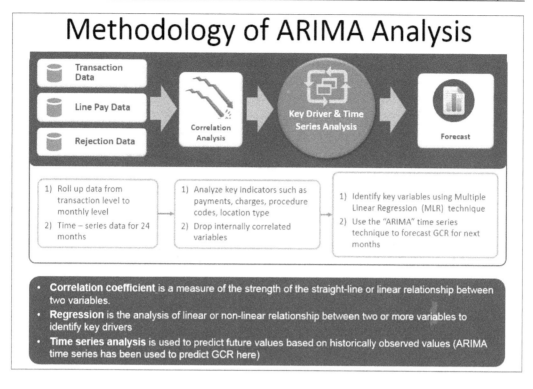

Methodology of ARIMA Analysis

Another way to look at time series data is through the classic time series equation, which is shown as follows:

$$Xt = mt + st + Yt$$

The preceding formula is defined as follows:

- *mt*: The component of trend (this changes slowly with time)
- *st*: The component of seasonality (for a given period); for example, look at the following:

  $d = 24$ (this is hourly),

  OR

  $d = 12$ (this is monthly)

- *Yt*: The component of random noise (the component of random noise might consist of various irregular but cyclical components that have completely unknown frequencies)

The following diagram shows the elements of a time series:

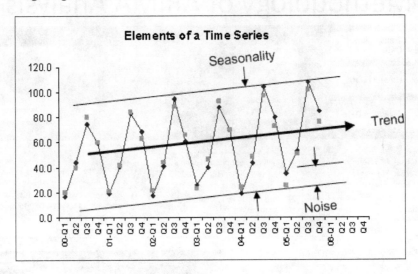

The following diagram shows you the different cycles in time series data. Hence, we have to take care of the cyclic behaviour of the data as well:

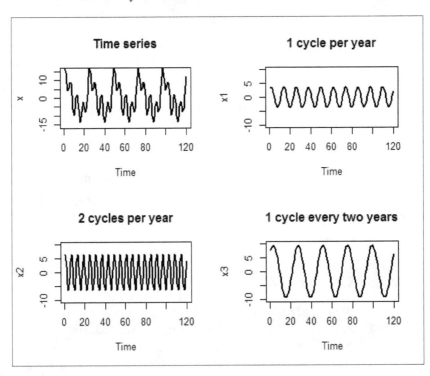

Code for time series analysis in Stata

Let's understand the Stata code to run the autocorrelation test first. To find autocorrelation, we draw correlograms. The command to draw correlograms is `corrgram`, for example, take a look at the following:

```
corrgram fridge_sales, lags(12)
```

You will get the following output when you run this command:

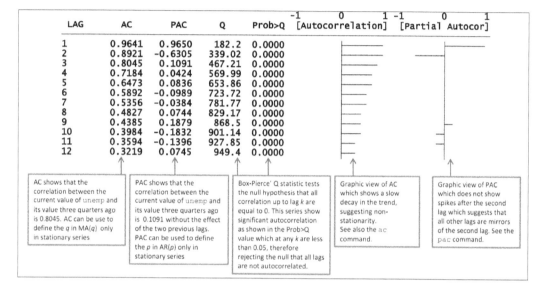

To explore the different relationships between two given time series, you can leverage the `xcorr` command.

The following graph depicts the existing correlation between the `fridge_sales` quarterly growth rate and volume. When you use the `xcorr` command, you need to type all the independent variables first, followed by the dependent variable:

```
xcorr fridge_sales volume, lags(10) xlabel(-10(1)10,grid)
```

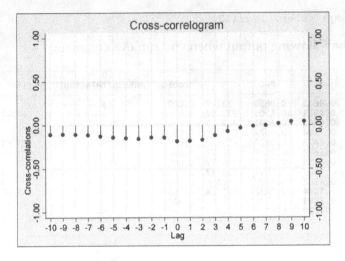

At *lag 0*, you can see that there is a nicely pointed out negative correlation between *fridge_sales* and the volume of the given model. This implies that the drop in volume causes a continuous and immediate increase in *fridge_sales*, as shown in the following table:

LAG	CORR	-1 0 1 [Cross-correlation]
-10	-0.1080	
-9	-0.1052	
-8	-0.1075	
-7	-0.1144	
-6	-0.1283	—
-5	-0.1412	—
-4	-0.1501	—
-3	-0.1578	—
-2	-0.1425	—
-1	-0.1437	—
0	-0.1853	—
1	-0.1828	—
2	-0.1685	—
3	-0.1177	
4	-0.0716	
5	-0.0325	
6	-0.0111	
7	-0.0038	
8	0.0168	
9	0.0393	
10	0.0419	

Now, let's check out the relation between `fridge_sales` and compressor efficiency:

```
xcorr fridge_Sales compressor, lags(10) xlabel(-10(1)10,grid)
```

The output of this command is as follows:

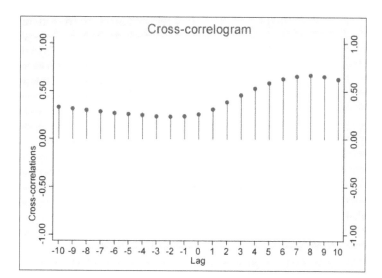

The code written at the beginning of the chapter produces the following output:

LAG	CORR	-1 0 1 [Cross-correlation]
-10	0.3297	
-9	0.3150	
-8	0.2997	
-7	0.2846	
-6	0.2685	
-5	0.2585	
-4	0.2496	
-3	0.2349	
-2	0.2323	
-1	0.2373	
0	0.2575	
1	0.3095	
2	0.3845	
3	0.4576	
4	0.5273	
5	0.5850	
6	0.6278	
7	0.6548	
8	0.6663	
9	0.6522	
10	0.6237	

Compressor efficiency has a very positive effect on the fridge sales for the given quarter, which reaches the highest tipping point at *lag 8*, as shown in the preceding diagram (which is also four quarters and 2 years). In this case, compressor efficiency is positively correlated to fridge sales but eight quarters later and after the introduction of the compressor in the market. This might be because the consumer is aware of the compressor efficiency of the new fridges after eight quarters compared to previous quarters; marketing campaigns too follow the time series pattern.

Way too many lags can increase the given errors for the forecasts created by ARIMA. In day-to-day work life, when your manager tells you to build the ARIMA mode, you can depend on the following three factors:

- Experience
- Knowledge
- Theory

The three most commonly leveraged indices to make sure that the ARIMA results are right are as follows:

- **Schwarz's Bayesian information criterion (SBIC)**
- **Akaike's information criterion (AIC)**
- **Hannan and Quinn's information criterion (HQIC)**

You can find these indices by leveraging the `varsoc` command, which is available in Stata:

```
varsoc fridge_sales compression, maxlag(10)
```

The output of this command is as follows:

```
Selection-order criteria
Sample:  1959q4 - 2005q1                      Number of obs      =      182
```

lag	LL	LR	df	p	FPE	AIC	HQIC	SBIC
0	-1294.75				5293.32	14.25	14.2642	14.2852
1	-467.289	1654.9	4	0.000	.622031	5.20098	5.2438	5.30661
2	-401.381	131.82	4	0.000	.315041	4.52067	4.59204	4.69672*
3	-396.232	10.299	4	0.036	.311102	4.50804	4.60796	4.75451
4	-385.514	21.435*	4	0.000	.288988*	4.43422*	4.56268*	4.7511
5	-383.92	3.1886	4	0.527	.296769	4.46066	4.61766	4.84796
6	-381.135	5.5701	4	0.234	.300816	4.47401	4.65956	4.93173
7	-379.062	4.1456	4	0.387	.307335	4.49519	4.70929	5.02332
8	-375.483	7.1585	4	0.128	.308865	4.49981	4.74246	5.09836
9	-370.817	9.3311	4	0.053	.306748	4.4925	4.76369	5.16147
10	-370.585	.46392	4	0.977	.319888	4.53391	4.83364	5.27329

Let's take a look at the following command:

```
regress fridge_sales compression if tin(1965q1,1981q4)
```

The output of this command is as follows:

Source	SS	df	MS				
Model	36.1635247	1	36.1635247		Number of obs =	68	
Residual	124.728158	66	1.88982058		F(1, 66) =	19.14	
					Prob > F =	0.0000	
					R-squared =	0.2248	
Total	160.891683	67	2.4013684		Adj R-squared =	0.2130	
					Root MSE =	1.3747	

unemp	Coef.	Std. Err.	t	P>|t|	[95% Conf. Interval]	
gdp	-.4435909	.1014046	-4.37	0.000	-.6460517	-.2411302
_cons	7.087789	.3672397	19.30	0.000	6.354572	7.821007

Now look at the following command:

```
regress fridge_sales compression if tin(1982q1,2000q4)
```

The output of this command is as follows:

Source	SS	df	MS				
Model	8.83437339	1	8.83437339		Number of obs =	76	
Residual	180.395848	74	2.43778172		F(1, 74) =	3.62	
					Prob > F =	0.0608	
					R-squared =	0.0467	
Total	189.230221	75	2.52306961		Adj R-squared =	0.0338	
					Root MSE =	1.5613	

unemp	Coef.	Std. Err.	t	P>|t|	[95% Conf. Interval]	
gdp	.3306551	.173694	1.90	0.061	-.0154377	.6767479
_cons	5.997169	.2363599	25.37	0.000	5.526211	6.468126

You can also check Durbin-Watson statistics and make sure that Durbin-Watson statistics are close to *two* in order to make sure that your ARIMA model is accurate. The standard error of the model should be as close to *zero* as possible.

Summary

This chapter covered time series concepts such as seasonality, cyclic behavior of the data, and the autoregression and moving averages methods. Also, we learned how to apply these concepts in Stata and conduct various statistical tests to make sure that the time series analysis that you performed is correct. Last but not least, this chapter showed you how to build time series prediction models that can be leveraged when your manager at work or your professor at school tells you to build a time series model.

In the next chapter, we will study survival analysis, which is heavily used in many industries, such as healthcare, mechanics contact centers, and marketing.

9

Survival Analysis in Stata

Survival analysis is also known as event analysis. It is used extensively in different fields, such as biomedicine, engineering, and social science. However, it is used for different purposes in different fields. For example, in biomedicine, it is used to analyze the time of death of patients and also for laboratory tests. In social science, it is used to analyze time events, for example, marriage, job verification, child birth, the call waiting time in call centers, and so on. In the engineering field, it is used to find out the breakdown time of machines. Survival analysis is also called reliability or failure time analysis.

When data is analyzed through old-style statistical models (for example, multiple linear regressions), a few features of survival analysis data (for example, censoring and non normality) might create hurdles. The non-normality feature interrupts the normality notion/assumption of a statistical model (for example, regression, Anova, and so on); a censored observation is a type of observation that has incomplete information. Basically, censoring has four forms, which are right truncation, left truncation, right censoring, and left censoring. Right censoring is used more often due to different reasons. In many data analyses, right censoring works effectively. For researchers, out of all the four types, right censoring can be easy to use, provided you understand it deeply. The main task of survival analysis is to track issues as well as note the time of interest. Often, this does not happen due to various reasons. One of the reasons for a drop in studies is unrelated studies, for example, a patient moving to a new place and not providing the new address. In short, all these examples of study will gradually observe the time of events.

In this chapter, we will cover the following topics:

- Survival analysis concepts
- Applications and code for survival analysis in Stata

Survival analysis concepts

Often, subjects are randomly entered, and this continues until the study is finished.

Hazard rate is another significant feature of survival analysis. Through hazard rate, anyone can find out the exact time from the given data. An example of discrete data is large intervals (months, years, and decades). In other words, hazard rate (discrete time) defines the probability, which an individual knows for an event at time t, and in doing so, an individual's life may be in danger. In short, hazard rate is the unseen rate for any event. To explain this further, let's consider a few examples. If hazard rate is constant and equal to 2, it means that in one unit, two events will occur in the given time interval, which is one unit longer than usual. In another case, let's consider that one person's hazard rate was 3.2 and the other person had 3.4 at the same time t; this means that the other person's high event risk was two times higher than the first one. Though hazard rate is an unseen/unobserved variable, it regulates the occurrence as well as the time of events; it is also the basic dependent variable in survival analysis.

Shape is another vital concept of hazard functions because they will have an effect on other variables, for example, survival functions. As we can see, the first graph on the next page of the hazard function has a U shape; this represents the hazard function of the liver transplant patient's survival time. At *zero* time, patients are have a *high* hazard function rate as the operation is very risky and there are more chances of dying. The chances of dying are a little less in the first 10 days of the operation compared to the actual operation time, where the chances are very high; thus, the hazard function rate declines. However, if the patients survive within 10 days of the operation, then they start getting back into shape; hence, they have less chances of dying in the next 6 months. On the other hand, if the patients' health starts falling (after 6 months), chances of dying will increase; as a result, the hazard rate will also increase. Later on, in the following year, if all patients are dead, then the hazard function will rise and will continue to rise.

The hazard function derives many functions, for example, the survival function; however, it does not look like an interesting variable. In short, the hazard function is the base component of all variables because once we have this function, other functions can be derived easily from the following code:

```
use http://www.mathminers.com/stata.dta,
clear gn id = ID1 drop ID1 stwset time,
failure(censor) sts1 graph0,
na
```

Or you can use the following code:

```
use stata1.dta,
clear gn id = ID1 drop ID1 stwset time,
failure(censor) sts1 graph0,
na
```

The output of this code is shown in the following figure:

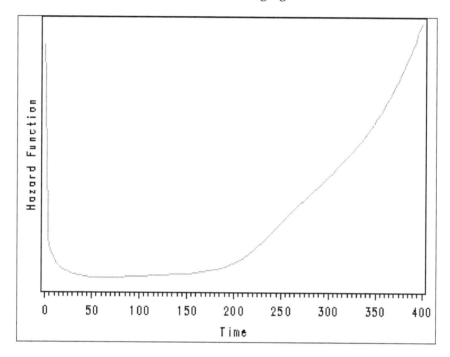

The following diagram shows the different stages and use cases of survival analysis in a statistical way. It talks about survival analysis, the hazard model, and sampling, and tries to come up with different insights:

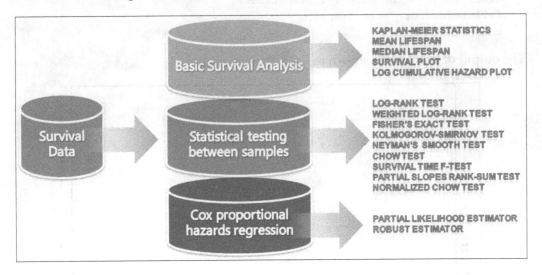

Applications and code in Stata for survival analysis

The main objective of the HEDIS data is to predict in how much time the patient will go back to drug use after taking medicines. Here, we have divided the patients into two groups and have given two different lines of treatment: *medicine=0* for short term and *medicine =2* for longer term. The patients were divided into two sets: *set=0* is set *a* and *set= 1* is set *β*. In the following table, variable *age = enrollment age*, *medth= methodus*, and *glycol= glycomet* used by patients in the last 4 months. The *medth1* variable denotes methodus use/glycomet use and *medth2* denotes either methodus or glycomet use; however, *medth3* denotes neither methodus nor glycomet use. The *metfomindrug* variable denotes the past medicine used and the line of treatment. The variable *time* denotes the times in which the patient goes back to the drug use, and the patient response denotes whether the patient came back. Patient *response1* denotes a return to medicine use and patient *response0* denotes that the patient will not return to drug use.

Now, we will move on to the top observations of the HEDIS data; note that subject 6 is patient response and has no event. The coding for the patient response is known as **counter-intuitive** because value 1 denotes an event, whereas value 0 denotes patient responsiveness. It may also be called a **variable event**.

	id	time	Age	metfordrug	medicine	sets	methdoux
1	1	120	20	7	0	1	4
2	2	10	30	1	0	1	5
3	3	108	35	2	1	1	2
4	4	234	50	6	0	1	6
5	5	774	59	25	0	1	1
6	6	54	18	2	0	1	4
7	7	640	45	45	0	1	7
8	8	44	65	4	1	1	9
9	9	410	80	8	1	1	5
10	10	150	79	9	1	1	3
11	11	310	70	1	1	1	1
12	12	501	60	8	0	1	2

Let's take a look at the following figure:

Building a model

In order to build a model, we will incorporate all regular predictors as well as predictors that have a lesser value of p (0.3-0.35). As methodux consists of three steps, the preceding predictor will be incorporated along with a dummy variable as well as methodux1 as a reference. A dummy variable can be formed through the xi command with Toxiq:

```
Toxiq age metfordrug j.sets 1.metho, Lsssdzc

Fail_c: patient response
Analysis_tm: time

Iteration 0: log Likelihood = - 38645.678, Iteration 1: log Likelihood
= -38546.876
Iteration 2: log Likelihood = -38546.956, Iteration 3: log Likelihood
= -38546.567

Refined estimate: Iteration 0: Log Likelihood  = -38456,567

Cox regression -- Breslow method
Total subjects- 520
Total observations - 520
Failures - 294
Risk time - 13259
Log likelihood - -38456.567          LRRRchiiirl(3) - 36.90
                                     Prob> chiiiir(3) = 0
```

t_time	Coefficient	Standard Error	y	P> !y!	[93% Conff interval]	
age	-0.12456	0.00654322	2.56	0.0001	-0.23456	-0.007654
metfordrug	0.24567	0.0056789	3.58	0.002	0.145678	0.3459898
1. med	0.356789	0.0876512	0.367	0.004	0.3456323	0.6745623
1.set	0.156438	0.20108791	1.96	0.079	0.2367529	0.01587654
methoduxxx						
2	0.342671	0.132568	1.02	0.0055	0.0054618	.5467890
3	0.2134569	0.1040654	2.12	0.3224	0.0897651	.2345679

```
test 2.methoduxxx
test 3.methoduxxx
(1) 2.methoduxxx = 0
(2) 3.methoduxxx = 0
chirrrr ( 2) = 5.354
Prob > chirrrrr 2 =0.2345
```

From the preceding code, we can see that the predictor `methodux` is not very important, but the the predictor site is essential in the model. So, we will remove the `methodux` predictor and the predictor site will remain in the final model. Hence, the final model will have the `Toxiq age metfordrug j.sets` effect:

```
Toxiq age metfordrug j.sets 1.methoduxxx, Lsssdzc
Failures :ces_censor
Analysis time dd_t: dt_time
Iteration 0: log likelihood = - 38645.678
Iteration 1: log likelihood = -385447.987
Iteration 2: log likelihood = -385446.657
Iteration 3: log likelihood = -385345.876
Refining estimates:
Iteration 0: log likelihood = -385345.876


Cox regression -- Breslow method is used for ties


Total subjects = 521
Total observation = 521
Total failures = 495
risk time    = 132765
LR chirrrr(4)  =23.54
Log likelihood  = -385345.876
```

t_time	Coefiecient	Std. Error	y	P> !y!	[93% Conff interval]
age	-.0331549	.00654908	-3.45	0.004	-.045689 -0.006754
metformindrug	0.0268907	0.006589	-.3.98	0.003	- .567890 -0.0776598
1. med	-.3456908	.0804560	-1.98	0.009	-.4568923 -0.5578900
1.set	.2345670	.2456098	-2.96	0.086	-.2987609 0.03456789

```
Prob > chirrrr2 = 0.0000
```

Proportionality assumption

The Cox Hazard proportionality model has a very significant feature called **proportionality assumption**. There are numerous ways through which we can verify that a particular model fulfills the proportionality model. However, in this case, we will examine proportionality by incorporating time-dependent covariates, such as vcr and temp in the stocx command. Here, predictors as well as time are the interactions of time-dependent covariates. In the present case, interaction is used along with log because generally, this function is used more frequently, yet apart from this, one can use any other function. Note that if a time-dependent covariate is important, then it disobeys the proportionality assumption of that predictor. To summarize, we can say that all time-dependent variables support the proportionality assumption hazard:

```
Stcox age metfordrug j.med j.sests ccs.age j.sests nmohrr vmcr

(age metfordrug medicinet ssets) temp(lmlnn(_tnt))

failure _d:  censor
analysis time _t: time
Iteration 0: log likelihood = -386446.552
Iteration 1: log likelihood = -386435.222
Iteration 2: log likelihood = -386335.333
Iteration 3: log likelihood = -386225.111
Iteration 4: log likelihood = -386225.111
Refining estimates: Iteration 0:

log likelihood = -386225.111

Total subjects = 510
Total observations = 510
Total failures = 390
Risk time    = 142994 132765
LR chirrrr2(9) =     23.456
Log likelihood = -386225.111
Prob > chirrrrr2 = 0.0000
```

_ttt	Coefficient	standard error	Z	p!z!	93% coeff interval
mainnn					
age	-0.0246799	0.024569	-0.87	0.254	-.087564 .0254678
metfordrug	0.0276588	0.2543789	0.65	0.645	-0.03528 .0702035
j. treatment	-0.554370	0.3225678	-1.54	0.201	-2.34568 .2030548
j.sestss	-1.54389	0.2111679	-3.21	0.017	-3.87657 - .2458769

_ttt	Coefficient	standard error	Z	p!z!	93% coeff interval
sests@age	0.0224567	0.025678	4.2	0.02	.002654 0.034678
vcr					
age	-0.0003067	0.006589	-0.007	0.866	-.0158787 0.0156743
metfordrug	0.0025678	0.00456389	0.72	0.638	-.0082456 .0165432
treatment	0.075478	0.07689	2	0.446	-.0721458 .1654337
sets	0.06789	0.087654	0.9	0.2789	-.107789 -.3678980

In the preceding table, the variables in the vcr equation interact with Imnln(_tnt).

The Schoenfeld and Scaled Schoenfeld residual is also one of the types to measure proportionality assumption. However, we have to first save the data using the stocx command. Through the Stphtest command, we can get the proportionality of the entire model, and a detail option is used in order to know the test proportionality of every predictor in the same model. A graphical representation of Schoenfeld can also be performed through the plot option. A proportionality assumption can be possible in the preceding table if the test result (*p* values above *0.006*) is not important. Additionally, in the following graph, the horizontal line depicts that we have not violated the proportionality assumption. In the current case, the stphplot command is used; in order to test the proportionality, this command uses the log-log plot. When we get parallel lines, it means that there is no violation in the proportionality assumption being done through predictors using the following code:

```
quietly stsscox age1 nnndurugtx treatments
sites d.age#j.site, schoenfeld(scsh*)
scaledsch(sca*) stphtest, detail stphtest, plot(age) msym(oh) stphtest,
plot(ndrugtx) msym(oh) stphtest, plot(treat) msym(oh) stphtest, plot(site)
msym(oh) stphtest, plot(c.age#1.site) msym(oh)  stphplot, by(treat)
plot1(msym(oh)) plot2(msym(th)) stphplot, by(site) plot1(msym(oh))
plot2(msym(th))  drop sch1-sch5 sca1-sca5
stphplot, by(treat) plot1(msym(oh)) plot2(msym(th)) stphplot, by(site)
plot1(msym(oh)) plot2(msym(th))  drop sch1-sch5 sca1-sca5
```

The test of the proportional hazards assumption is as follows:

	cdgee	chirrr	difference	prob>chirrr
age	0.12346	0.06	2	0.56789
metformindrug	0.04657	2.34	2	0.114561
treatment	0.20987	3.56	2	0.124352
sets	0.34256	0.34	2	0.536719
age_sets	0.025467	0.07	2	0.66543
global testing		7.35	10	0.32456

The graph for this data is as follows:

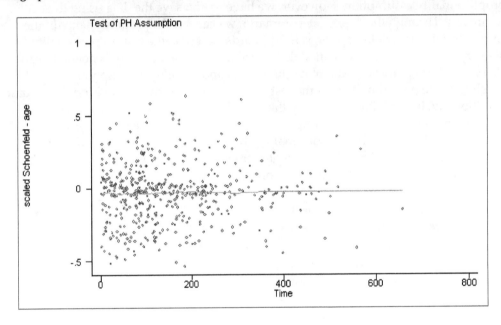

The graph for `ndrugtx` is as follows:

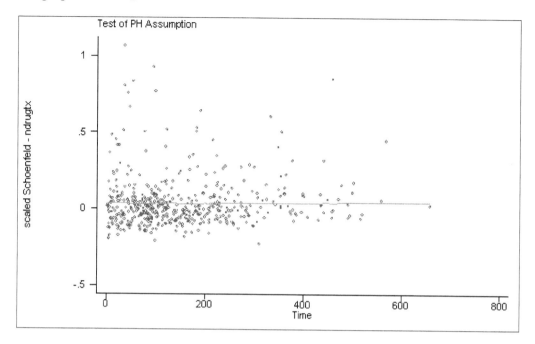

The graph for `treat` is as follows:

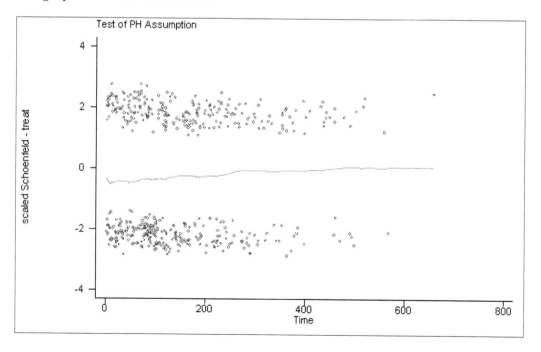

The graph for `site` is as follows:

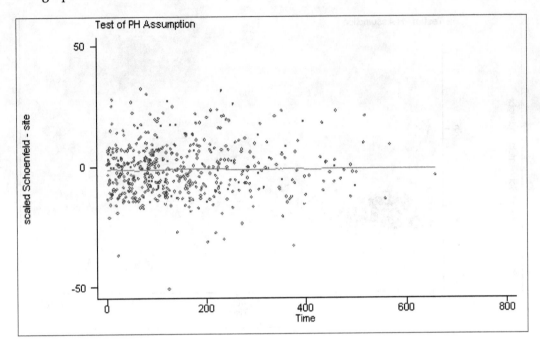

The graph for `age_site` is as follows:

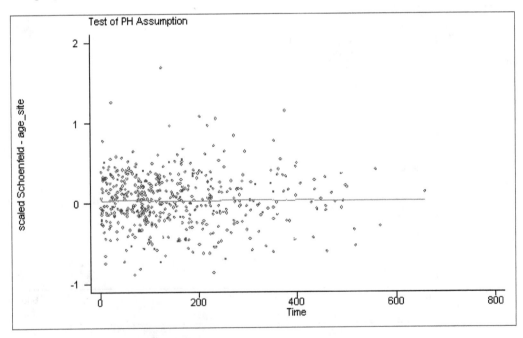

The graph for `treat` is as follows:

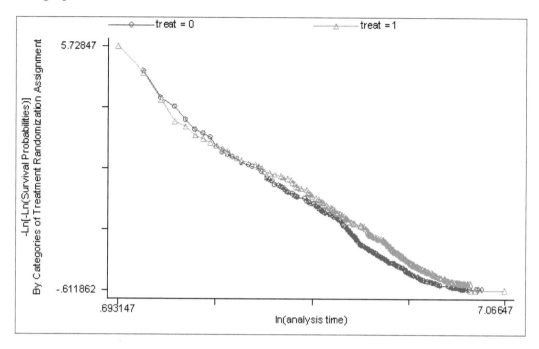

The graph for `treat` is as follows:

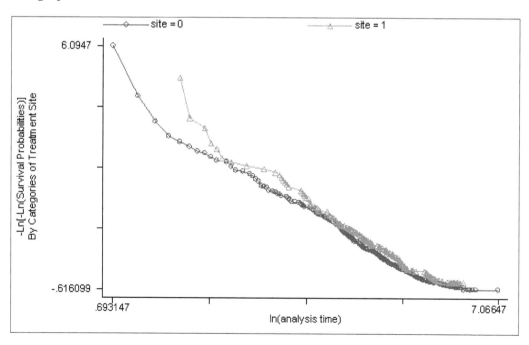

The code to create the preceding graphs is as follows:

```
bysort treat: stcox age ndrugtx site c.age#i.site, nohr

Treat = 0
Failures _dt: censor dtt
Analysis_time _ttt: time
Iteration 0: log likelihood = -1.23.1145
Iteration 1: log likelihood = -1204.5678
Iteration 2: log likelihood = -1204.6356
Iteration 3: log likelihood = -1204.5437
Refining estimates: Iteration 0:
Log likelihood = -1204.5437

Cox regression - Breslow method is used for ties

Total subjects = 220
Total observations = 220
Total failures = 140
Risk time = 55466
LR chirr (4) = 14.15
Log likelihood = -2.453786
Prob > chirr = 0.0014
```

Here is how you can use survival analysis to build churn models:

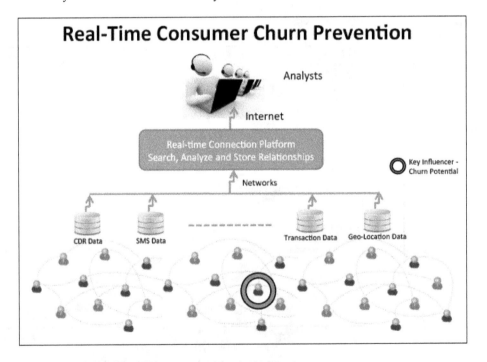

Summary

This chapter teaches the concepts and the applications of survival analysis in detail. On a general note, it is assumed that survival analysis is used only in biostatistics. However, this chapter shows that it can be used in other industries as well in order to build churn models, among others.

This book walked you through various analytical techniques in Stata. An important point of this book is to not only make you familiar with Stata, but also with statistical analytics methods.

Index

H

heteroscedastic **86**
histograms
  defining 46
homoscedasticity
  defining 86-88
Huynh-Feldt (H-F) test **69**

I

IF
  used, for data file 13-15
IM test
  about 87
  measures 87
IN
  used, for data file 13-15
indicators
  defining 12
infix command **10**

J

jargon **90**

K

Kernel density estimation (KDE) **56**

L

linear regression
  code, in Stata 78-84
  defining 75-77
  types 76, 77
line plots
  defining 43-46
local macros **6**
logistic regression
  defining 89, 90
  for finance (loans and credit cards) 106
  in Stata 94-105
  logit 90-92
  requirements 91
  types 98

logit
  about 90
  log odds 90
  odds 90
  odds ratio 90
  Ormcalc command 90
  probability 90
loops
  defining 32-34

M

macros **6, 29-31**
MANOVA
  defining 69-71
matrices **6**
moving average process (MA) **125, 126**
multicollinearity **85, 86**
multivariate analysis of
        variance. *See* **MANOVA**

O

odds ratio command **90**
one-way MANOVA
  defining 69
Online Linguistic Support (OLS) **89**
options, Stata
  clear option 9
  delimiter option 9
  option name 9

P

pie charts
  defining 49
placeholder **13**
proportionality assumption **142**
pyramidal graphs
  defining 50, 51

R

residual variance **86**

S

sampling fraction 111
scatter plots
  defining 37-43
simple random sample (SRS) 112
Stata
  about 1, 6, 17
  absolute path 7
  commands 6
  curve fitting 60
  data management 2
  data, reading 7
  data-storing techniques 6
  data visualization 2
  directories 6, 7
  folders 6, 7
  infix command, using 9, 10
  insheet 8, 9
  linear regression 2
  logistic regression 3
  loops 32-34
  macros 6
  matrices 6
  relative path 7
  Stata programming 2
  statistical tests 2
  Stat/Transfer program 10
  survey analysis 3
  survival analysis 3
  time series analysis 3
Stata graphics 37
Stata interface
  defining 4, 5
statistical calculations
  defining, in graphs 53-59
Statistical Package for the Social
      Sciences (SPSS) 1
Stat/Transfer program
  copying and pasting 11
  defining 10
  typing 11
survey analysis
  defining 107-111
  in Stata code 112-118
  primary sampling unit 108

stratification 109
  weights 107, 108
survival analysis
  about 135
  applications and code 138
  concepts 136-138
  model, building 140, 141
  proportionality assumption 142-148

T

tab 8
tabulated reports
  preparing 20-25
time series analysis
  about 123
  ARIMA 123
  autoregressive (AR) process 124, 125
  concepts 123
  elements 127
  moving average process (MA) 125, 126
  Stata code 129-133
t tests
  defining 63, 64
  two independent sample t tests 64, 65

V

variable event 138
variables
  defining 11
  labeling 17-19
variable transformations
  labeling 17-19
variance inflation factor (VIF)
  about 85
  using 85
vioplot command 52
vio plots
  defining 51

W

while loops
  defining 35, 36
Wilcoxon-Mann-Whitney test
  defining 72, 73

Thank you for buying
Data Analysis with Stata

About Packt Publishing

Packt, pronounced 'packed', published its first book, *Mastering phpMyAdmin for Effective MySQL Management*, in April 2004, and subsequently continued to specialize in publishing highly focused books on specific technologies and solutions.

Our books and publications share the experiences of your fellow IT professionals in adapting and customizing today's systems, applications, and frameworks. Our solution-based books give you the knowledge and power to customize the software and technologies you're using to get the job done. Packt books are more specific and less general than the IT books you have seen in the past. Our unique business model allows us to bring you more focused information, giving you more of what you need to know, and less of what you don't.

Packt is a modern yet unique publishing company that focuses on producing quality, cutting-edge books for communities of developers, administrators, and newbies alike. For more information, please visit our website at www.packtpub.com.

About Packt Enterprise

In 2010, Packt launched two new brands, Packt Enterprise and Packt Open Source, in order to continue its focus on specialization. This book is part of the Packt Enterprise brand, home to books published on enterprise software – software created by major vendors, including (but not limited to) IBM, Microsoft, and Oracle, often for use in other corporations. Its titles will offer information relevant to a range of users of this software, including administrators, developers, architects, and end users.

Writing for Packt

We welcome all inquiries from people who are interested in authoring. Book proposals should be sent to author@packtpub.com. If your book idea is still at an early stage and you would like to discuss it first before writing a formal book proposal, then please contact us; one of our commissioning editors will get in touch with you.

We're not just looking for published authors; if you have strong technical skills but no writing experience, our experienced editors can help you develop a writing career, or simply get some additional reward for your expertise.

Tableau Data Visualization Cookbook

ISBN: 978-1-84968-978-6   Paperback: 172 pages

Over 70 recipes for creating visual stories with your data using Tableau

1. Quickly create impressive and effective graphics which would usually take hours in other tools.

2. Lots of illustrations to keep you on track.

3. Includes examples that apply to a general audience.

Statistical Analysis with R

ISBN: 978-1-84951-208-4   Paperback: 300 pages

Take control of your data and produce superior statistical analyses with R

1. An easy introduction for people who are new to R, with plenty of strong examples for you to work through.

2. This book will take you on a journey to learn R as the strategist for an ancient Chinese kingdom!

3. A step by step guide to understand R, its benefits, and how to use it to maximize the impact of your data analysis.

4. A practical guide to conduct and communicate your data analysis with R in the most effective manner.

Please check **www.PacktPub.com** for information on our titles

Practical Data Science Cookbook

ISBN: 978-1-78398-024-6   Paperback: 396 pages

89 hands-on recipes to help you complete real-world data science projects in R and Python

1. Learn about the data science pipeline and use it to acquire, clean, analyze, and visualize data.

2. Understand critical concepts in data science in the context of multiple projects.

3. Expand your numerical programming skills through step-by-step code examples and learn more about the robust features of R and Python.

R for Data Science

ISBN: 978-1-78439-086-0   Paperback: 364 pages

Learn and explore the fundamentals of data science with R

1. Familiarize yourself with R programming packages and learn how to utilize them effectively.

2. Learn how to detect different types of data mining sequences.

3. A step-by-step guide to understanding R scripts and the ramifications of your changes.

Please check **www.PacktPub.com** for information on our titles